I Love INDIA

Anjum Anand

Recipes and stories from city to coast, morning to midnight, and past to present

Photography by Martin Poole

quadrille

SATHI
LASSI

CONTAINS
YAHOURT
SUGAR
CREME
HONEY
SAFFRON
CARDAMOY
CASHEWNUT
PISTACHIO
RAISINS
MOTOR BIKE ON RENT

Contents

Introduction

I believe that each of us is the sum of all our parts. I know that everything I have done and experienced in life has brought me to this place in my career and, looking back, I see how all the dots join up. In my case, these indelible markers started before I did.

My father was born in India towards the end of the British Raj, only 12 years before the Partition. His family were enjoying a cool break in Kashmir when they received word that the rumours about India splitting were indeed true, and that they had to gather what they could and travel to find a new home within the new Indian borders. This was a time of utter chaos, confusion and fear, with people traversing whole countries with more apprehension than belongings. My father's family travelled on the top of a train for days, slept in a railway station for weeks and – with lots of help from old friends – made their way to Delhi. Many months later, they finally settled into a new home and life. By the age of 18, my father got a job with a British company, which meant he got the opportunity to travel a little. In his early twenties – for the second time in his young life – he moved to a new country where he knew no one and had little more than a few coins in his pocket.

My mother grew up in the mountains between Afghanistan and what is now Pakistan. She had six sisters and one brother and grew up very sheltered, her older sisters more like mothers to her. They were a proud family, with a little land to their name. My grandfather was a trader, importing fruits and nuts into India from Afghanistan. My mother's extended family had more advance warning about Partition and came to live with my grandfather's brother in a large, sprawling family home in Old

Delhi. In time, the home was split between the men of the family, while all the women married and left for their new families' homes. By the time I visited this imposing villa, my mother's brother lived in a one-bedroom flat with his wife and children (space for the new families having diminished as children arrived). It was small, but the grounds of the house were huge, with flat roofs forming verandahs around the home; everyone was surrounded by family and cousins, and all the positives – and the politics – that that involved.

My parents had an arranged marriage. My father travelled to India and met my mother; five days later they were married and he brought her to London… a world as different from hers as it was distant. The way she remembers it, my father had a party at home in London to celebrate his marriage and to introduce his new bride to his friends. My mother had never before been out without her sisters or cousins and she apparently left the party – full as it was of drinking, smoking and the loud friends of my father – and sat on the doorstep, looking at the stars, with tears falling for all she had left behind and apprehension for what was to come.

By the time we were born, my mother had settled into her new role as a supportive wife and – by the time I was four – my father decided to move us to Switzerland. We spent ten years in Geneva, the weekdays in school and the weekends driving around exploring a completely new world and cuisine. We went from one recommended restaurant to another, acquiring a taste for everything Swiss and middle European – with a bit of German, French and Italian – fondue and raclette, *filets de perches* (a local river fish), *spätzle* (a short noodle-like dumpling), Birchermüesli, wild strawberries and raspberries, pâtisserie and, of course, amazing cheeses and chocolates. Swiss food is very good; often simple but rich.

Inside our Swiss home, it was more akin
to a little India, with Indian food on the
table and Indian movies playing on the
television, instead of the local networks.
My father's new circle of friends was also
Indian as, having spotted a Sikh man at
the bus stop, he went straight up to him,
introduced himself and soon met all the
other Indians in the small city.

My father loves having people round and
these new friends were often invited over
for dinner, so I have countless memories
of women dressed in colourful saris with
clinking bangles, laughing and recounting
stories from "back home", eating Indian
food that Mum had spent the day cooking
(enlisting a very eager young me to help)
and generally giving me the impression that India
was an amazing, vibrant, fun place full of interesting characters.

This was only reinforced on the frequent trips we took to India. In the
early days we stayed with family, only taking hotel rooms once my father
could afford them. One of his cousins had a chicken farm and, on arrival,
we would receive a basket of eggs and have the tastiest eggs on toast.
The food in India was always amazing; I don't remember a single bad
meal. Visits to my father's family were always meaty affairs, with melting
mutton curries and soft, puffed
chapatis anointed with a little ghee.
In contrast, my mother's family
were vegetarian and preferred
lighter food and meals that usually
featured lentils with seasonal
vegetables and some of their own
specialities. These meals were

often punctuated with fresh sugar cane brought in from a nearby field; we would sit and use our teeth to strip off the hard fibrous "skin", tear off large chunks, chew the flesh, extract all the sweet, flavourful juices and spit out the fibrous remains into a large bowl.

My mother's family were wonderful vegetarian cooks, but she herself cooked to feed her carnivorous husband and children. For ten years she even took to eating meat to be more accommodating… before finding her voice and reverting to her own style of food. She had always wanted to work, but my father wanted a more traditional wife who took care of the home and children. She would say to me that, despite my interest in the kitchen, girls with a good education and opportunities could be anything they wanted to be (though when we didn't help, she couldn't stop herself from saying that if we didn't cook no one would marry us!). I agreed and didn't even think about pursuing cooking professionally. My father's life seemed much more exciting; he ran his own business, travelled and was always surrounded by friends.

But two years after completing my business degree and working in a small company, reality dawned… I wasn't enjoying any of it. The only thing that gave me any pleasure was cooking for myself after I got home from work. I had returned to the kitchen after a prolonged absence to cook myself low-fat Indian food. By this point, I had been on countless diets

and, although I lost weight, it always returned. I realized the only way to keep the weight off was to enjoy the Indian food I loved, but in a lighter, lower-fat guise than that I had been eating. So I started learning my favourite dishes properly and cooking them for myself regularly. Cooking became my main passion and, with prompting from a few friends, I realized I didn't have to force myself to stick doggedly to my career path; I remembered I could do anything I wanted to do… and I wanted to cook.

I tried everything. I worked in both a fast-food place and an Indian restaurant in New York, both as waiting staff and as an apprentice in the kitchen. I worked in a hotel kitchen and at a catering company… generally in any job I could get that had some exposure to a kitchen. The more experience I got, the more I worked in the kitchen.

I found that my driving force was dispelling the myth that Indian food was unhealthy, and full of ghee and nut pastes; in reality, Indian food is fresher, tastier, lighter and more varied than most people realize. It became a bee in my bonnet whose buzzing became too loud to ignore… and I decided to write my first book. That first book led to a BBC series: *Indian Food Made Easy*. I have since presented another couple of series and also launched a range of Indian foods called The Spice Tailor. My impulse is always the same: to bring authentic regional Indian flavours to everyone. Ironically, my life now does mimic my father's and – now that I am a mother myself – my mother's as well.

One of the questions I am asked the most (even by my mother!) is where I get my inspiration to write book after book on Indian food. That is the easy bit. I have been very lucky to have spent months and months in India, travelling and eating, talking and learning about the regional food. I have countless memories of eating chaat on the streets with my cousins and, later, kebabs on the streets with my friends, eating in the homes of friends from different communities, dining in some of the best restaurants and *dhabas* (simple streetfood-style cafés) around the country. I have eaten dishes that we have never heard about outside of India, such as spicy meat pickles; curries made from sorrel; puffed, roasted and spiced lotus seeds; smoked naans; water chestnut curries; and sweets made from almost everything. I have tasted Indian dishes inspired by Moghuls, Turks, British, Portuguese, and Arab traders, and Chinese immigrants.

I married a British Indian with a Rajasthani heritage and bonded with my mother-in-law (an amazing cook) over her son's favourite dishes from that region. I have been to some of India's most spiritual temples and enjoyed the purest vegetarian meals, where the food feels almost blessed by its closeness to places of good energy.

I have a passion for Indian food that surpasses all others. It comes from a combination of learning more about the country of my heritage, respecting its amazing and ancient cuisine that accepts all new influences and adopts them with no prejudice. I love the fact that people cook and eat together and – of course – I love the flavours and feel healthy when eating them.

I might not have been writing my eighth book if all my dots had not led me to this point. I have filled this book with my fondest food memories of India, and have relived so much of my life as I have written the recipes down. It is my favourite book so far, perhaps because it is the one that speaks the most of all my experiences and shows you a little – through the dishes I have inherited and discovered – of who I am.

Street-side tiffin

The streets of India are vibrant, chaotic and colourful places. Homes are often small, so a lot of life takes place on the neighbourhood thoroughfares. A walk down the road often entails bumping into children making their way to school; witnessing early morning washing being hoisted up on the balconies to dry in the hot, emerging sun; hearing snatches of conversation as news is exchanged while sipping glasses of tea; or jumping out of the way of deliveries being made on cycles, wooden carts or on the back of a tempo (a small, open-backed truck). All the while, there is the background smell and sizzle of Indian streetfood.

India's streetfood is basically fast food that is affordable and really, really delicious. Most cities in India don't have a main shopping street; instead, shops and stalls tend to cluster in little self-contained markets, selling everything from saris to jeans and sneakers, bindis (the colourful dots some women wear on their foreheads), bangles, shoes, books, sunglasses and more, all interspersed with the mouthwatering streetfood of the region.

The range of streetfood in India is astonishing, from simple dishes such as seasonal vegetables doused in lemon juice, seasoning and chilli powder, or cool lassis in the summer, to warming chai and samosas in the winter. More substantial bites can come in the form of fresh-grilled meat wraps, stir-fried vegetables with buttered buns, fried battered fish, steamed dumplings with a broth, chaats (a genre of Indian streetfood) of all kinds, pakoras and freshly made flatbreads. And the city streets remain alive with life and food late into the night, catering for everyone from couples out for a stroll who might want a cooling ice cream or syrup-doused shaved ice cones, to late-night revellers who get hungry after a night on the town. Indian streetfood is as bountiful, dynamic and exciting as the street life itself.

When I was in my late teens, I went to Mumbai to stay with a friend and – the morning after a long evening out – her mother asked us what we had got up to. When she heard that we'd eaten kebabs and wraps in a very famous late-night streetfood place, she told us off… not about late nights out but about eating streetfood in India! The truth is that many echo her thoughts, and that it is a quick way to pick up something nasty. I think this is one of the main reasons that streetfood came into the domestic kitchen.

Even though India is opening up and embracing Western coffee bars and burger joints, thankfully most still crave the Indian flavours they grew up with. In this chapter, I have chosen some of my favourites. Many can double up to be served as a light meal, but all are streetfood-inspired and delicious!

I would never go to Delhi without visiting Sunder Nagar market to eat a plate of this famous streetfood. The hawker tosses crispy papri into a dried banana leaf plate, tops with potatoes and chickpeas, and almost throws the yogurt on and – lastly – the chutneys. All the while, I watch, mesmerized; there is something so relaxing about those deft, repetitive moves.

It is hard to understand how such humble ingredients create such a spectacular mouthful, delivering so many flavours and textures. I don't know anyone who doesn't gravitate to this dish. I make it often, and you can buy both the papri and the tamarind chutney, so there is little work involved. This is mostly a lunch or teatime snack for us, though we also make it when friends come over. You can also make more elegant bites using pani puri, the spherical papri, and stuff them as on page 48. **Serves 4–6**

Delhi papri chaat

For a traditional plating, place the papri, slightly overlapping, on a platter. Scatter over the potato and chickpeas.

Whisk the yogurt with the spices, sugar and salt. Spoon evenly over the discs and then spoon over both chutneys (normally they are just spooned over but you can try drizzling them over in lines, or even feathering them with a toothpick).

Scatter over the onions, sev and pomegranate seeds, if using. For fingerfood-type bites, serve individually, with all the bits crowning each papri. Serve immediately.

15–20 large 7.5cm (3in) papri
  (fried pastry discs)
1 waxy potato, boiled, peeled and
  cut into 2cm (¾in) cubes
2 handfuls of cooked chickpeas
  (garbanzo beans), rinsed if canned
250–300g (1–1¼ cups) plain
  yogurt, ideally full-fat
½ tsp chaat masala
¾ tsp roast and ground cumin seeds
  (see page 184)
pinch of chilli (chili) powder
  (optional)
good pinch of sugar
good pinch of salt
3–4 tbsp tamarind chutney (bought,
  or for homemade see page 181)
3–4 tbsp Tangy Herb Chutney
  (see page 182)
2 tbsp finely chopped red onions
large handful of sev (small crispy
  vermicelli), if you can find it
handful of pomegranate seeds,
  to serve (optional)

I sought out my first vada pau as I had been hearing about it for years and couldn't understand how a potato burger could have so many fans. I was sent to a little roadside stall in Pune, a couple of hours' drive from Mumbai. I ordered one, paid 10 INR (10 pence/cents) and waited. I was soon joined by a crowd of working men, all placing their orders. It all happened in minutes: balls of the spiced mashed potatoes were dipped in the batter, fried, then, almost faster than the eye could see, they were drained and slapped into rolls already smeared with chutneys and wrapped in paper. They were handed over, the server remembering exactly who had ordered what and how many. The vada pau was so much tastier than I had imagined – light, almost melt-in-your-mouth, with a lightly crisp coating, and the chutneys added so much complexity. My vada pau is inspired by that first experience. **Makes 8**

Maharashtra's ultimate potato burger

Bring a big pot of salted water to the boil. Halve the potatoes and cook until soft. Leave to cool, then peel and mash.

Meanwhile, heat 1½ tbsp oil for the filling in a small pan. Add the mustard seeds and, when they start to pop, throw in the curry leaves. Follow after a few beats with the ginger, garlic and chilli and cook, stirring often, until the garlic smells cooked, around 1 minute. Add the turmeric, stir for 10 seconds and take off the heat. Add the cool mashed potato, lemon juice, coriander and salt to taste and mix it all together; I use my hands as I find it all comes together better. Taste and adjust if necessary. Make into 8 roughly equal-sized balls.

Whisk together the ingredients for the batter, adding a good pinch of salt and enough water to make a medium-consistency batter (40–50ml/ 3 tbsp). The thinner the coating, the lighter and crispier it will be.

Slice the buns in half, but not all the way through. I like to toast them in a hot oven or a frying pan, but they can just be at room temperature.

Heat 10cm (4in) of oil in a wide saucepan, karahi or wok over a medium heat; the oil needs to be medium hot. Taking 1 ball at a time, flatten it gently into a burger shape (I like the centre to be slightly thicker than the edges). Place in the batter and, once well coated, place straight into the hot oil. Repeat with another 2. If the potatoes are not completely submerged in the oil, using a slotted spoon, quickly splash hot oil on top so it seals. Cook until golden and crisp on both sides. Place on kitchen paper and repeat to cook the remaining burgers.

As these cook, spread the herb chutney on one side of the bun and sprinkle the dry chutney on the other (you can also make a paste of this by adding some water). Place the potato burgers on the dry chutney side, close and enjoy.

For the filling
salt
500g (1lb 2oz) potatoes (around 2 large ones)
vegetable oil
½ tsp brown mustard seeds
12 fresh curry leaves
1½ tsp finely grated root ginger
1 large garlic clove, finely grated
1 Indian green finger chilli (chile), finely chopped, or as much as you like
⅓ tsp ground turmeric
1½ tsp lemon juice, or to taste
good handful of chopped coriander (cilantro)

For the batter
75g (⅓ cup) chickpea (gram) flour
¼ tsp baking powder

To serve
8 soft pau, burger buns or baps
8 tbsp Tangy Herb Chutney (see page 182)
6–7 tbsp Dry Garlic Chutney (see page 180)

Curry leaves

These lovely, droopy herb leaves – each with a sharp point and a vibrant, glossy green coating – rival coriander (cilantro) in India's food affections. Curry leaves are an essential ingredient and form part of the "Holy Trinity" of South Indian flavours, along with mustard seeds and coconut. Many people who live on the western coast will grow curry leaves in the garden, and pick stems off as needed. Contrary to their name, they don't smell of curry, but have a lovely, clear, identifiable aroma of their own.

You really don't need a reason to cook with these lovely leaves other than their sublime flavour but, according to ancient Indian medics, the herbs are a real powerhouse of health. They are believed to be anti-oxidant, anti-inflammatory, anti-fungal and anti-bacterial as well as being full of minerals and vitamins so – a bit like turmeric – they are a vital ingredient to include in the diet as often as possible. In Indian Ayurvedic medicine, curry leaves are believed to relieve congestion, detoxify the liver, stabilize insulin and blood sugar levels (so great for diabetics), be helpful for anaemia as their folic acid helps absorb iron, and be good for digestion and cholesterol levels. My father-in-law eats two or three curry leaves on an empty stomach with a couple of black peppercorns and a date every morning, as part of his health regime… his vitamins, so to speak!

On a cosmetic note, curry leaves are thought to be really good for bad skin and dry, damaged or limp hair: you blend a good handful of the fresh leaves, heat them gently with some cosmetic oil, then massage into the skin or hair as necessary.

To get the best out of curry leaves, they only need to be fried in a little oil to release their inherent flavour, then be cooked until lightly crisp. Unfortunately, fresh curry leaves don't keep for long, so when you buy a batch, wrap what you think you might use (still on their stems) in moist kitchen paper and keep them in the fridge. Dry the rest on baking sheets and then store in an airtight container; they won't have as much flavour, so use them with a heavier hand, but they will still liven up any dish.

This Gujarati favourite – handvo – has crispy edges and a soft, vegetable-laden interior. It is normally made from lentils and rice, ground into a paste and fermented overnight, but this is an instant version. It is packed full of vegetables, as well as protein from the chickpea flour, flax and pumpkin seeds. You can change the vegetables, and leave out one or both of the seeds if you don't have them at home. This would be eaten as a snack with a cup of tea, but it makes a lovely lunch with some salad, or is great on a picnic, or even as a savoury breakfast. Traditionally, this was always made on the hob but most Gujuratis I know now bake this in the oven as it is an easier and more efficient way to do it. I sometimes miss the crust, so add those bits in later, under a grill or on the hob. **Makes 8 generous wedges or 10 smaller squares**

Savoury courgette, seed and curry leaf cake

Mix together the semolina, chickpea flour, milled flaxseed, yogurt, onion, ginger, peas, chilli, salt, turmeric and most of the water. Allow to rest for 30 minutes.

Preheat the oven to 200°C/400°F/gas mark 6. Oil a 23cm (9in) springform baking tin and line the base with parchment paper.

Coarsely grate the courgette, squeeze out the excess liquid and add to the mix. Taste and adjust the seasoning if necessary.

Heat the oil in a small frying pan and add the mustard seeds and cumin seeds. Once the mustards seeds are popping, add the curry leaves, sesame seeds and sunflower or pumpkin seeds and cover the pan, as these will puff up and jump. Once the sesame seeds are golden, take off the heat and add two-thirds of the contents of the frying pan to the batter. Adjust the water if necessary until the batter has a thick pouring consistency. Stir in the bicarbonate of soda.

Pour the batter into the prepared baking tin, cover with foil and bake in the oven for 20 minutes. Remove the foil and continue to bake for 10 minutes, or until the batter is cooked through and a cocktail stick (toothpick) comes out dry. Take out of the oven. For a crispy top, brush and scatter over the remaining oil and seeds and place the cake on the upper oven shelf for a few minutes. It should be a lovely deep golden.

Cool a little before slicing and serve as it is, or with Tangy Herb Chutney (see page 182). If you are making this in advance, you can always toast the upper side in a frying pan until golden and crisp and scatter over the remaining seeds at that point.

165g (1 cup) fine or medium-grain semolina
35g (¼ cup) chickpea (gram) flour
1 tbsp milled flaxseed
120g (½ cup) plain yogurt
½ small red onion, finely chopped
10g (2 tsp) finely grated root ginger (peeled weight)
70g (½ cup) frozen peas, defrosted
½–1 Indian green finger chilli (chile), finely chopped
1 tsp salt, or to taste
½ tsp ground turmeric
200ml (⅞ cup) water
1 courgette (zucchini)
3½ tbsp vegetable oil, plus more for the skillet or tin
1½ tsp brown mustard seeds
1½ tsp cumin seeds
small fistful of curry leaves
2½ tbsp sesame seeds
1 tbsp sunflower or pumpkin seeds
⅓ tsp bicarbonate of soda (baking soda)

Momos are a Nepalese dumpling similar to a Chinese one, but made with Nepalese/Indian ingredients. Calcutta is full of momo houses and, whenever I go, I have to eat in them at least once. You are given a menu full of options, steamed and pan-fried and stuffed with as many fillings as the chef can imagine, everything from mutton to vegetables – even paneer. The traditional dipping sauce recipe I give here is fiery and tomato-ey, but I often mix some finely chopped ginger, garlic and green chillies into soy sauce and that normally hits the spot without much fuss. Momos are easy to make, fun and really satisfying.

The dough can be made in advance, but will soften as it sits. You can form the momos just before your friends arrive and have the steamer ready and the kettle boiling so, when your friends are settling in, all you need to do is light the flame. **Makes 24**

Steamed Nepalese meat momos

Mix together all the ingredients for the filling. (You can fry a little of it to test the seasoning, if you like.) Cover and leave this one to rest for 1 hour in the fridge.

For the dough, mix the flour and salt together in a large bowl and add the water slowly, mixing well to create a medium-stiff dough. Knead well and add a little more water if the dough splits. Cover with a damp dish towel, or wrap in cling film (plastic wrap), and leave to rest for 20 minutes.

Take out the dough and knead well again. Roll it into 2 long sausage shapes about 2cm (¾in) in diameter. Mark the halfway point with a knife and then further mark each half into 6 sections, giving you 24 equal pieces.

Cut one sausage of dough at a time, covering the remainder each time to prevent the rest drying out. Roll each piece out thinly, on a lightly floured surface, into a 7.5cm (3in) circle about 1mm (¼in) thick.

Place 1½–2 tsp of the filling into the centre of each skin. I hold the momo in my left hand with my thumb on the stuffing. With my right hand I seal the tops together, folding a little as I go. My thumb from the left hand presses the filling down to make sure there is none in the sealed edges. Basically, you need to enclose the filling in the dough without any tears; you can do it any way which feels easy.

Oil the surface of a steamer basket, or line with greaseproof paper. Arrange the momos on the oiled surface as you make them, leaving some space between them as they expand a little. Cover and steam on a rolling boil for 11–13 minutes. Serve immediately with Spicy Charred Tomato Chutney.

For the filling

250g (9oz) minced (ground) pork, lamb or chicken thigh

10g (½ packed cup) coriander (cilantro) stalks and leaves, finely chopped

handful of green peas, defrosted (optional)

¼ small red onion, finely chopped

20g (⅙ cup) spring onions (scallions), finely chopped

½–1 tsp green chillies (chiles), finely chopped

3 large garlic cloves, finely grated or finely chopped

15g (1 tbsp) finely chopped root ginger (peeled weight)

¾ tsp garam masala (fresh if possible, see page 113)

2 tsp dark soy sauce

¼ tsp freshly ground black pepper

2 good pinches of salt

vegetable oil, for the steamer basket (optional)

Spicy Charred Tomato Chutney (see page 181), to serve

For the dough

100g (¾ cup) plain (all-purpose) flour, plus more to dust

good pinch of salt

5 tbsp cold water, plus more to seal

My husband's family are vegetarian and many of them are quite particular, so they wouldn't eat a vegetarian dumpling in most places as they are normally stacked and steamed on top of meatier ones. In Calcutta, restaurants know their customers and they have separate steamers for vegetarian and non-vegetarian dumplings. So when we go to momo houses there, the family happily ask for the vegetarian menu and go to town on a large variety of vegetarian options. I love a vegetable-based dumpling but I do sometimes miss the umami and meatiness of the original ones so I came up with the mushroom version. They are full of that savoury flavour that most vegetables lack. These are normally steamed, but I love them pan-fried, which gives them more texture and flavour. **Makes 18 medium-large momos**

Crispy pan-fried mushroom momos

For the filling, heat the oil in a medium non-stick saucepan. Add the onion and some salt and fry until the onion is soft and colouring. Add the ginger and garlic and cook for 40–50 seconds or until the garlic is cooked through. Add the mushrooms and soy sauce and cook until the mushrooms release water and then it dries up. Add the vinegar, black pepper and cornflour slurry and cook for 3–4 minutes or until there is no more moisture and the cornflour is cooked. Cool and stir in the spring onion, pepper and coriander. Adjust the seasoning.

For the dough, mix the flour and salt in a large bowl and add the water slowly, mixing well to create a medium-stiff dough. Knead well and add a little more water if the dough splits. Cover with a damp dish towel, or wrap in cling film (plastic wrap), and let rest for 20 minutes.

Take out the dough and knead well again. Roll it into 3 long sausages and cut each into 6 equal pieces. Roll each piece into a ball, covering the remainder each time to prevent them from drying out. Roll each ball out, on a floured surface, into a 6–7.5cm (2½–3in) circle.

To make the momos, place 1½ tsp of the filling into the centre of each skin. I hold the momo in my left hand with my thumb on the stuffing. With my right hand I seal the tops together, folding a little as I go. My thumb from the left hand presses the filling down to make sure there is none in the sealed edges. Basically, you need to enclose the filling in the dough without any tears; you can do it any way which feels easy.

At this stage you can freeze them or cook them straight way. Heat the oil for frying in a large non-stick frying pan that can hold all the momos (work in batches if necessary). Once the oil is hot, add the dumplings, pleat side up, turn the heat down to medium and cook for 2–3 minutes or until golden and crisp on the bottom. Add 100ml (6 tbsp) water from a just-boiled kettle and once steaming, cover and cook for 4 minutes. Uncover and cook on a high heat until the water evaporates, the momos crisp up on the bottom again and the upper edges are cooked through. Serve immediately with Spicy Charred Tomato Chutney.

For the filling

2½ tbsp vegetable oil, plus 1½ tbsp for frying

1 small-medium red onion, finely chopped

salt

15g (1 tbsp) finely grated root ginger (peeled weight)

6 large garlic cloves, finely chopped

550g (5 cups) finely chopped chestnut mushrooms

2 tbsp dark soy sauce

3 tsp white or red wine vinegar

1 rounded tsp freshly ground black pepper, or to taste

1½ good tsp cornflour (cornstarch), mixed into a slurry with 50ml (3½ tbsp) water

2 small spring onions (scallions), chopped

small fistful of freshly chopped coriander (cilantro)

4 tbsp finely chopped green pepper

Spicy Charred Tomato Chutney (see page 181), to serve

For the dough

100g (¾ cup) plain (all-purpose) flour, plus more to dust

good pinch of salt

5 tbsp cold water, plus more to seal

On the streets of Goa you will find stir-fried chilli beef dishes. The beef is already cooked with spices and local flavourings, then stir-fried to order and served with local bread: pau. I think they are even better with chorizo, with all the smokiness and spiciness those sausages bring. You can't get pau in the UK, but its softness is similar to that of burger buns – only with more structure and flavour. I also sometimes add some good-quality mayonnaise (mixed with some fresh chopped coriander and black pepper) for a bit of creaminess along with the rocket. **Serves 3 (can be doubled)**

Chilli-fried chorizo dogs

Add the oil to a frying pan, add the chorizo and onions and cook gently until the chorizo releases oil and the onions are starting to soften. Add the chillies and stir-fry for a few minutes, then throw in the tomato and a splash of water, increase the heat and cook until the tomatoes have softened and the whole thing comes together.

Serve hot in the buns, with a little rocket, if you like.

1 tsp vegetable oil

250g (9oz) raw chorizo sausages, sliced

2 small red onions, thinly sliced

3–4 Indian green finger chillies (chiles), stalks removed, pierced with a knife

1 medium-large tomato, finely sliced

3 hot dog buns, or other longish bread rolls, split lengthways

handful of rocket (arugula, optional)

I have had too many late nights out in Bombay to count. We used to spend at least one week a year there at Christmas, mostly with friends from London who have roots there and a kicking social life. After a long night out we used to go to a kebab place called Bade Miyan, which roughly translates as "the elder gentleman" or "head honcho". To us, it meant succulent kebabs of all types, plain or in breads. This went on until my friend's mother found out we were eating there and told us we could get kidney failure! I have no idea why... but we did stop going soon after. Those days have gone, but my love of streetfood remains.

This baida roti is fairly easy to make at home and hits the spot after a night out. A tasty, tasty meal. You can make it with minced chicken or Quorn instead, but you will need to cook the onions until golden first, then add the ginger and garlic, then the rest of the ingredients and cook until done. **Serves 2**

Mumbai roadside hot lamb sandwich

Heat half the oil in a large frying pan, add the onion and cook for 3–4 minutes, then add the minced meat, garlic, ginger, chilli, tomato, spices and salt. Bring to a simmer, then cover and cook until the meat is soft and the excess liquid has evaporated, giving the pan an occasional stir and breaking up the meat; it might take 15–20 minutes or so. Drain off any excess fat, tip into a bowl and leave to cool, wiping the pan.

Meanwhile, make the dough. Add the salt to the flour, with the oil and around 60ml (¼ cup) water. Knead until smooth; it shouldn't be too soft. Cover with damp kitchen paper and leave to rest as the lamb cools.

Whisk the egg with a little salt and the coriander. Divide the dough in half, and roll out into 20–23cm (8–9in) squares or rectangles, trying to roll the outer 3cm (1¼in) border a little thinner than the rest.

Using the same pan that you have wiped, add the remaining oil and heat up gently.

Quickly make the stuffed rotis: place half the filling in the centre of each flatbread, leaving a 7.5cm (3in) border along the edges. Spoon 3 tbsp of the egg over each. Bring down the upper edge, fold in the sides and then the lower edge to enclose the filling, forming into a flat-ish square.

Place straight into the hot pan, seam sides down, and cook until golden on both sides. Serve hot with the chutney.

For the meat filling
2 tbsp vegetable oil
½ red onion, finely chopped
200g (7oz) minced (ground) lamb
  (or see introduction above)
3 large garlic cloves, finely chopped
  or grated
8g (½ tbsp) finely grated root ginger
  (peeled weight)
½–1 Indian green finger chilli
  (chile), finely chopped (optional)
1 small tomato, chopped
⅔ tsp ground cumin
½ tsp garam masala (fresh if
  possible, see page 113)
salt
1 small egg
handful of chopped coriander
  (cilantro) leaves

For the wrap and to serve
salt
80g (⅔ cup) plain (all-purpose)
  flour, or chapati flour, or spelt
  flour (the first is traditional but
  I often use the others at home)
1 tsp vegetable oil
5 tbsp Tangy Herb Chutney
  (see page 182)

Flattened beaten rice, or poha, is eaten in so many parts of India, mostly for breakfast. I rarely have a savoury breakfast, but I love this as a light lunch. The rice is cooked and then beaten, so it is flat but with a soft, slightly chewy texture which is really lovely. This is fantastic: full of lovely textures and really easy to make. Potatoes are typical, but you can leave them out if you are in a hurry, or add another vegetable instead. At home, I often add some chopped beans, peas and cauliflower florets so that I have had my vegetables. Unlike a lot of other poha dishes, this one is more characteristic of streetfood because it has a lot of garnishes. You can add as many or as few as you like, although the more you add, the tastier it will be. **Serves 1 with leftovers, or 2 as a light meal**

Spiced, flattened rice with potato

Heat the oil in a frying pan. Add the mustard and fennel seeds and reduce the heat. Cook until they are popping, then throw in the chillies and curry leaves and cook for a further 20–30 seconds. Add most of the onion, leaving 1 rounded tbsp to serve, add some seasoning and cook until the onion is golden on the edges.

Meanwhile, place the poha in a sieve and wash in water for about 1 minute. Leave it in the sieve to soften.

Add the potato, turmeric and some more salt to the onion and sauté for a few minutes, then splash a little water into the pan, bring to a simmer, cover and cook for 5–7 minutes, stirring often, or until the potatoes are just cooked through.

Add the peanuts and poha and stir well to incorporate. Add a good squeeze of lemon juice – around 2 tsp or to taste – and the coriander leaves, if using. Taste and adjust the salt, adding the sugar, and serve sprinkled with the sev, the remaining chopped onion, coconut and/or pomegranates, if using.

1½–2 tbsp vegetable oil
⅓ tsp brown mustard seeds
¼ tsp fennel seeds
1–2 small Indian finger green chillies (chiles), stalks removed, halved lengthways
10 fresh curry leaves
1 small red onion, finely chopped
salt
180g (1 cup) flattened rice (poha), ideally a thick variety (they come in different thicknesses)
1 small waxy potato, peeled and cut into 1cm (½in) cubes
¼ tsp ground turmeric
2 tbsp roasted peanuts
½ small lemon
½ tsp sugar, or to taste (optional but traditional)

For the typical garnishes
some chopped coriander (cilantro)
good handful of sev (small crispy vermicelli)
freshly grated coconut
pomegranate seeds (optional)

Poha: flattened rice

Also called *poya* or *powa* in different regions, this is a par-boiled rice that has been flattened and then dried. Poha is fluffy, has a light chew and takes just a few minutes to steam through. It is one of India's favourite breakfasts when lightly stir-fried with mustard seeds, curry leaves and some simple vegetables. The resulting meal is really delicious and nutritious… but it won't weigh you down.

It is also fried and served in a salted nut and raisin mix like a sweet-salty Bombay mix (very addictive!). Many will use it in desserts cooked with a little jaggery, or made into a kheer. I absolutely love poha but, as I don't normally do savoury breakfasts, I mostly eat it in a light lunch pilaf, or as part of a meal. It is definitely worth trying; everyone who has tried it once loves poha.

Goan food is heavily influenced by their former Portuguese colonizers, so there is a love of pork, pastry and vinegar, as well as beef, that is not found in other regions. These little pies are inspired by the pork empanadas much loved in Goa. I have changed the pastry as I wanted to bake rather than fry these pies, and also altered the recipe a little texturally, though the flavours are fairly true to the original. These are best served hot and make a wonderful lunch with salad, or are great for picnics, or also amazing as finger food (though you might want to make them smaller). **Makes 8 medium or 10 small pies**

Goan pork pies

Start with the pastry. Place the flour and salt in a bowl. Add the butter and rub in with your fingertips until the whole thing looks like crumbs; don't overwork it, or the pastry will be tough. Add the egg yolks and ice-cold water and bring together only until it is smooth and not cracking too much. The heat of your hands will help this. Make the dough into a smooth log, wrap it in cling film (plastic wrap) and place in the fridge to firm up and settle for 1 hour. (You can do this the night before, but take out and allow to soften before rolling.)

For the filling, heat the oil in a large non-stick saucepan. Add the onions and cook until they are soft and well browned on the edges. Meanwhile, blend the ginger and garlic into a paste, adding enough water to help the blades turn. Scrape into the cooked onions and stir until all the liquid has dried off and the paste has had a chance to fry a little. Add the pork, flour, chillies and spices and stir over a gentle heat for a few minutes. Pour in the chicken stock and seasoning and bring to the boil. Cook over a medium heat for 20–25 minutes, or until the pork is soft.

Add the sugar and vinegar, then take off the lid and stir to evaporate most of the liquid; the filling should be moist. Remove the chillies, stir in the coriander and leave to cool.

When ready to cook, preheat the oven to 180°C/350°F/gas mark 4. Take the pastry out of the fridge and cut into 8 pieces. Allow to soften slightly if they are hard. Using a little flour, roll each one out into a roughly 10cm (4in) circle. They are quite delicate as they are quite short, so don't press too hard. Place a rounded tbsp of filling, plus a bit more, in the middle, brush milk all around the edge and enclose to make a semi-circle. Press the edges together to seal, either with your fingers or with the tines of a fork. Place on a baking sheet lined with greaseproof paper or foil and buttered. Repeat to form all the pies.

Brush well with the beaten egg, leave to settle, then brush again with egg. Place on the middle shelf of the oven and bake for 20–25 minutes, or until golden. Serve hot or warm.

For the pastry
225g (2 scant cups) plain (all-purpose) flour, plus more to dust
¼ tsp salt
90g (6 tbsp) cold unsalted butter, chopped, plus more for greasing
2 egg yolks
3 tbsp ice-cold water
a little milk
1 large egg, lightly beaten

For the filling
3–4 tbsp vegetable oil
2 medium-small red onions, finely chopped
30g (2 tbsp) chopped root ginger (peeled weight)
40g (1½ oz) garlic cloves
400g (14oz) pork shoulder, finely chopped (around ½–1cm/¼–½in)
1 tbsp plain (all-purpose) flour
3–5 green chillies (chiles), stalks removed, pierced with a knife
1 rounded tsp garam masala (fresh if possible, see page 113)
1 rounded tsp ground cumin
½ tsp ground turmeric
1 tsp Kashmiri chilli (chili) powder
300ml (1¼ cups) chicken stock
salt and freshly ground black pepper
1½ tsp sugar, or to taste
about 2½ tbsp white wine vinegar
handful of coriander (cilantro), finely chopped

"Chaat" is a term used for a whole genre of streetfood which is hard to describe in one sentence, but one part of it encompasses a lot of simple vegetables and fruits tossed in some tangy and spiced lemon-based dressings with a blend of spices that are known as chaat masala. "Chaat" literally means to lick, as in finger-licking good... and they generally are. This chicken chaat is based on the one we ate growing up but we normally had it as a chopped salad, so everything mixes well with the tangy dressing. For a proper salad (rather than a streetfood snack), I like to serve it on a plate, drizzled with lots of dressing for that real chaat flavour. If you have friends round, serve on fried tostadas (flour tortillas, cut into small rounds and deep-fried until golden), drizzled with a little Tangy Herb Chutney (see page 182) mixed with some crème fraîche, or in tacos with the same chutney and sour cream. Scatter with pomegranate seeds for sweet fruitiness. **Serves 1 as a light meal, 2 as a starter, or 6 in lettuce leaves as a nibble**

Griddled chopped chicken salad

Marinate the chicken breast with 1 tsp of the olive oil, seasoning and the garlic. Leave for 30 minutes if possible.

Heat a griddle pan or frying pan, add the chicken and cook for 5–6 minutes on each side or until done. I like to cover the pan (with another pan) 2 minutes in, to keep the chicken moist.

Meanwhile, mix together the remaining olive oil, seasoning, roast cumin and a little each of the coriander and lemon juice.

Chop the tomato and avocado into even 1–2cm (½–¾in) cubes. Place in a bowl and add the onion, lettuce, chaat masala, chilli and most of the dressing. Toss well to mix and season to taste. It should be tangy, spicy and well-seasoned. Add more lemon juice if necessary.

When the chicken is done, you can slice it thinly and place on top of the salad, drizzled with the remaining dressing and remaining coriander, or chop into small bites and mix with the salad, dressing and remaining coriander. I also like the flavours to marinate for a bit before serving, so make it up 10–15 minutes before serving if possible.

Scatter over the peanuts and serve.

1 large skinless chicken breast
1½ tbsp extra virgin olive oil
salt and freshly ground black pepper
1 large garlic clove, finely grated
1 tsp roast and ground cumin seeds (see page 184)
good fistful of chopped coriander (cilantro), finely chopped
1½ tbsp lemon juice, or to taste
½ medium-large tomato
½ ripe avocado
¼ red onion, finely chopped or thinly sliced
handful of chopped lettuce, such as Little Gem
1½ tsp chaat masala
¼ small Indian green finger chilli (chile), deseeded and thinly sliced
1½ tbsp salted peanuts, lightly chopped

There are so many wraps in India these days, but the original is probably the one made in Calcutta at the Nizam kebab shop. A customer was in a hurry – everything that a kebab was served with was thrown into an Indian flatbread – and a legend was born. They brushed egg over one side of the flatbread (and cooked it out), probably to seal the bread and prevent it from becoming too soggy quickly, but it does also add another flavourful element. You can add it in or leave it out as you like. The papaya paste helps to tenderize meat but, if you marinate it overnight, it should still be soft. Obviously, these make great kebabs without the wrap for friends, for a barbecue, or just for the carb-conscious. **Makes 3 (can be doubled)**

Grilled lamb kebab kathi rolls

Start with the marinade. Whizz together the yogurt, ginger, garlic, quarter onion, chilli, spices, salt, lemon, papaya and vegetable oil together until smooth. Add the lamb and leave to marinate for at least 1–2 hours; or overnight, covered, in the fridge, is best.

When you are ready to eat, heat the fan-assisted grill (broiler) element of your oven to high. Oil a baking sheet and place it on the middle shelf to heat up. Place the kebabs straight on the sheet, or skewer them first if you prefer. Cook for 8–9 minutes, or until the tops are charred and the meat is cooked through to your liking. They should be soft and flavourful. If you can do this on a barbecue, it will be even better.

Meanwhile, salt the sliced onions and add a good squeeze of lemon juice. Beat the eggs lightly with a little salt.

Heat a non-stick frying pan over a medium-high heat and add 1 tsp of oil. Brush a good amount of egg on the surface of your wrap and place egg side down in the hot oil. Once the egg is cooked, flip over and add one-third of the lamb, onions, tomato and chutney. Take off the heat, wrap and serve. Repeat to make the remaining kathi rolls.

Stand-alone creamy kebabs

The little elements I suggest here take these delicious kebabs to a new level and I often make them this way. It is inspired by a kebab made in Hyderabad.

Blend 8 mint leaves into the marinade with the remaining ingredients. Soak 2 tsp white poppy seeds (or 1 rounded tbsp cashew nuts) in 1 tbsp water for 15 minutes, then pound or blend to a smooth paste. Add to the kebabs after they have marinated. Dry roast 2 tbsp chickpea (gram) flour in a frying pan until it becomes grainy, darkens a few shades and smells roasted. Add to the kebabs as well. Cook as above. This will give the kebabs a lovely creamy, flavourful coating. Serve with lemon juice or Tangy Herb Chutney.

For the marinade

100g (⅖ cup) plain yogurt

10g (2 tsp) finely grated root ginger (peeled weight)

3 large garlic cloves

1 red onion: halved and one half sliced

½–1 Indian green finger chilli (chile), stalk removed

good grinding of freshly ground black pepper

1½ tsp garam masala (fresh if possible, see page 113)

¾ tsp ground cumin

1 tsp salt

1 tsp lemon juice

½ tsp grated green papaya (see introduction above), peeled before grating (optional)

2 tbsp vegetable oil, plus more for oiling and to cook the rolls

For the kebabs

250g (9oz) young lamb, cut into 2.5cm (1in) cubes

squeeze of lemon juice, plus 1 lemon, cut into wedges

2 eggs

3 wraps (try a simple paratha – page 195 – or one of the other flatbreads in the book)

1 tomato, sliced

3 rounded tbsp Tangy Herb Chutney (see page 182)

I visited the city of Amritsar a few years ago, full of anticipation as it was my first ever trip to Punjab. The people are friendly, proud and well-mannered and the food is delicious and honest. They put the tastiness of their dishes down to the sweetness of their water. Very humble of them, as their food is so delicious.

I had eaten Amritsari fish before but never in Amritsar itself, so eating this in as many places as I could find became a bit of a mission. My version is based on my favourite one there from a restaurant called Makhans. The fish is cooked like chips. It is partially deep-fried and then deep-fried again as it is ordered. This ensures a lovely, crisp batter. I don't do this at home, but for that extra crispness, that is the trick. We eat these with drinks, with some Tangy Herb Chutney (see page 182) but for a proper meal, I enclose it in a wrap with chutney and crunchy vegetables. **Serves 4 as a light meal with salady bits**

Amritsari fried fish

Place the fish in a non-metallic bowl.

Make the marinade by blending the ginger, garlic, lemon juice, salt to taste, pepper, chilli powder, cumin and turmeric to a fine paste (you might need to add 1–2 tbsp water, to help the blades turn). I do this in my powerful blender and the paste is nice and fine; just get it as fine as you can. Stir in the carom seeds. Taste and season well, spoon over the fish and toss well to coat completely and evenly. Leave to marinate for 1 hour.

Mix the chickpea flour with the rice flour, a good pinch of salt and the cumin seeds. Add about three-quarters of this to the fish and toss well to coat. Leave for 5–6 minutes; the water from the marinade will help it stick. If not, add a little water in.

Place the rest of the chickpea flour on a plate and toss the fish on this to coat on both sides, in case there are some bald bits.

Heat 7.5–10cm (3–4in) of oil in a large wok, karahi or saucepan, or deep fat fryer until hot; the temperature should be around 180°C (350°F) on a kitchen thermometer, or until a piece of the batter sizzles immediately. Add a batch of fish pieces, but do not overcrowd the pan; they should sizzle immediately. Fry until golden brown and crisp, 4–5 minutes. Remove with a slotted spoon and place on kitchen paper to blot off excess oil while you cook the next batch.

Sprinkle over the chaat masala and serve immediately.

For the fish
400g (14oz) firm white fish fillets
    or loins, cut into large chunks
    (I use sea bream; in Punjab they
    use river fish)
150g (1 generous cup) chickpea
    (gram) flour
3 tbsp rice flour
½ tsp cumin seeds
vegetable oil, as needed
1 rounded tsp chaat masala

For the marinade
20g (1½ tbsp) chopped root ginger
    (peeled weight)
25g (scant 1oz) garlic cloves
3 tbsp lemon juice
salt
¼ tsp freshly ground black pepper
¾ tsp chilli (chili) powder, or to
    taste
1 rounded tsp ground cumin
½ tsp ground turmeric
¾ tsp carom seeds

It is often just me at home – or only me who wants to eat healthily, anyway! – so I have a whole batch of dishes I go to. I do love sprouts as they are healthy, have a lovely nutty texture and can be cooked in minutes. It is common in India to sprout your own beans. Washed mung beans (mostly) are placed in wet muslin (cheesecloth), which is then tied and left for 1–2 days until the beans sprout. It is as easy as that, though you might need to rewet the cloth. Once sprouted, these are lightly cooked and used in many different ways. This is one of my favourite, quick, easy and tasty ways of using them. You can also buy sprouted beans from some supermarkets and many healthfood shops. **Serves 1 (can be doubled)**

Sprouted beans, curry leaves and coconut

Blend together the tomato, coconut, cumin and coriander seeds (if using), with the help of a little water to help the blades turn, until smooth.

Blanch the sprouts in boiling water for 2 minutes, strain and set aside.

Heat the oil in a non-stick frying pan. Add the mustard seeds and, as they pop, add the curry leaves and dried chilli. Follow 5 seconds later with the onion and some salt. Sauté until deep gold in colour. Add the blended coconut mixture, the ground coriander, if using, and a little more salt and cook over a high-ish flame until the masala releases oil into the pan, around 5 minutes.

Add the sprouts and a splash of water, bring to the boil and simmer for 1 minute. Taste and adjust the seasoning and serve sprinkled with more coconut and the chopped coriander.

½ tomato, halved
40g (1½ oz) coconut, pieces or
  grated, plus 1 tbsp more to serve
½ tsp cumin seeds
1 tsp coriander seeds, or ground
  coriander
125g (4½oz) sprouted mung or
  mixed beans, washed
1 tbsp vegetable oil
⅓ tsp brown mustard seeds
8 curry leaves
1 dried chilli (chile)
½ onion, finely chopped
salt
chopped coriander (cilantro),
  to serve

Mustard seeds

Mustard seeds are the tiny dried seeds from the flower of the mustard plant. They come in three colours: brown, black and pale yellow. In India we tend to use the brown seeds most. On first inspection they have little aroma but, once fried, they have a lovely nuttiness and, when ground, a strong mustard pungency emerges.

The seeds are used abundantly around India, famously in the South Indian trinity with dried chillies and curry leaves; or ground and used to make pickles with seasoned vegetables. But perhaps the region most synonymous with mustard is Bengal, where you could be forgiven for thinking it was the national spice. The Bengalis feel about mustard the way Parsis do about eggs: there is no place they don't belong! This love of mustard makes Bengali food unique and delicious; in fact, I can see where the Brits got their love of mustard…

A word of warning: grinding brown mustard seeds can sometimes make them bitter. Soaking them in water first, then grinding them with green chillies and salt, is believed to remove that possibility, but – to be honest – I find this is also hit-and-miss, so I sometimes add ready-prepared mustard powder to a dish where a fresh mustard seed paste was the traditional ingredient. I also often grind a batch of dry brown mustard seeds and store them in a container to be quickly ground once again later, with other ingredients; for some reason, this tends to help.

Store mustard seeds in an airtight container, away from light, for a year or more. This spice goes with everything!

Sunset bites

Probably my first foray into cooking was making mini cocktail samosas for my parents' dinner parties. My father is from a region of India where, typically, dinner is served late and – in the interim – you sustain yourself on little canapé-type bites that are served with drinks. Indians don't really do starters, so these bites are generally inspired by some sort of streetfood, snack or anything that can be miniaturized and not interfere with the flavours of the main course. As I have grown older, I still find these the most fun things to cook and experiment with in the kitchen.

I lived in Spain for six months or so and I quickly subscribed to the tapas style of eating: small bites of varying textures, flavours and ingredients shared with friends over a long evening with a few drinks, and often replacing dinner. In fact, it is my perfect kind of evening, so much so that on the first night of my wedding (it lasted three days), we had a party for all of our friends to get into the spirit of things and get to know each other. I thought a constant stream of heavier canapés served through the night would be ideal. At around 11.30pm one of my close friends asked me what time dinner was going to be served, as she was saving her appetite and was now starving… as were, apparently, many others. I asked a waiter to bring out more food, but everything I ordered had been finished.

Embarrassed and concerned that people would be hungry at my party – a double insult as an Indian and a "professional" cook – I went straight to the kitchen. No one stopped me. There probably wasn't much precedent; as a hotel guest I was definitely not allowed in the kitchen, but I was the bride and clearly – many drinks in and in disbelief that they hadn't cooked enough – on a mission. We opened up the fridges and together mystery-boxed the contents to cook up some more food. It wasn't gourmet, but the guests left less hungry.

I don't think I have changed much since then. In fact, being around food a lot in the day, I like nothing more than to end a long week in a similar fashion. When friends come round, I often cook up a variety of filling, snacky, tapas-like bites for us to graze on through the evening as we sit around catching up with a bottle of something. I make sure there is a broad variety and that there is enough for everyone: some healthy bits, others heartier, some gluten-, carb- or dairy-free. There is only so much I can fit into one chapter, but you can "shrink" many other dishes in the book and serve them in this way. My only word of warning is this: let your friends know the plan, and make sure there is enough for the hungriest of guests; that way you can avoid spending precious friend-time in the kitchen, frantically scavenging through the contents of the fridge!

North Indians have a love of chaat, the finger-licking streetfood which comes in many guises. You wouldn't actually find this type on an Indian street, but it takes super-quick crisp baby spinach pakoras and mixes them with typical streetfood yogurt chaat-style ingredients. The resulting bite is crispy, hot, cold, creamy, herby and ever so tasty. Although this is deep-fried, it doesn't absorb a lot of oil and still feels fresh. When it is hot outside, I often chop up some frozen Tangy Herb Chutney (I always have some frozen, see page 182) instead of defrosting it and place little pieces on top; it looks better and is really interesting in the mouth. **Makes 10/ serves 5 (can be doubled)**

Crispy spinach chaat

Mix together all the dry ingredients for the chaat. Add 4 tbsp water and stir well, then put in the spinach and stir well to mix. It will be a bit gloopy.

Heat a large wok or karahi with 7.5–10cm (3–4in) of oil. When the oil is hot (around 180°C/350°F), or until a tiny piece of the spinach mixture sizzles straight away, take walnut-sized balls with your hands and flatten so they are 1–1½cm (¼–½in) thick. They will be irregular, which will help them be crispy. Add them all, then reduce the heat a little and fry until golden brown, turning occasionally. Remove with a slotted spoon and place on kitchen paper to blot off any excess oil.

To serve, whisk the yogurt with the roast cumin and salt it lightly. Place 2 spinach pakoras on to a small plate, I like to arrange them overlapping each other at an angle. Dollop over 2 tbsp of the yogurt, leaving the edges clear so they remain crispy. Spoon over 1 tbsp sweet tamarind chutney and 1 rounded tsp Tangy Herb Chutney. Sprinkle liberally with the sev or pomegranate seeds, if using, then serve.

For the chaat
50g (generous ⅓ cup) chickpea (gram) flour
1 tbsp cornflour (cornstarch)
⅓ tsp salt
¾ tsp ground coriander
½ tsp chaat masala
⅛ tsp ground turmeric
⅛ tsp chilli (chili) powder, or to taste
good pinch of carom seeds (delicious, but omit if you don't have any)
40g (1⅓ cups) baby spinach, really roughly chopped
vegetable oil, to deep-fry

To serve
150g (generous ½ cup) Greek-style yogurt
1 good tsp roast and ground cumin seeds (see page 184)
salt
5 tbsp sweet tamarind chutney (for homemade, see page 181)
5 rounded tsp Tangy Herb Chutney (see page 182)
sev (small crispy vermicelli, optional)
pomegranate seeds (optional)

Few people think of Indian food when they think of mussels, but they are loved on the west coast and take spices and strong flavours really well. They are cooked in curries, stir-fried in dry masala, enveloped in pastries, baked in tarts, steamed in "jackets" made from rice, stuffed and deep-fried... this is a typical mussel recipe from Kerala and is one of my favourite ways of eating it.

These are a sort of Indian tapas, good to pick at with some drinks. You can serve them however you like, in a big pile sprinkled with coriander and some lemon wedges, on little toasts brushed with coriander oil, or on the half shell on a bed of curry leaves. I always have a full larder, so it is easy for me to add semolina for a crunchy finish, but you can leave it out and it will still be divine. **Serves 4**

Crispy fried spiced mussels

Clean the mussels well by pulling off their rough "beards" and washing well in water; scrub them if they are muddy looking. If you find any which are open, tap them a couple of times on the sink: if they close, they are good to use; if they remain open, discard them.

Pour about 1cm (½in) of water into a large saucepan. Salt it lightly and bring to a simmer. Add the mussels, cover and cook for 2–3 minutes or until they have opened. Take off the heat and uncover. Start taking out the mussels from the shells as soon as they are cool enough to handle and place into a bowl. Add a couple of spoons of the liquor from the pan and toss with the ginger, garlic, spices and the ½ tsp salt. Set aside for 10–20 minutes.

Clean out the saucepan, or heat up a non-stick frying pan over a medium-high heat and add half the oil. Add the rice flour to the mussels and toss well to coat. Place the semolina on a flat plate and toss the mussels in this. When the oil is hot, fry a mussel until crisp on both sides, flipping once. Taste for seasoning and spice. If you need to add more of either, this is the best time to do it. Add 1 dried chilli and half the curry leaves to the pan and follow, after 10 seconds, with half the mussels. They should not overcrowd the pan. I like to cook these over a medium-high heat, flipping once, until crisp on both sides, just a few minutes. Spoon out into an open bowl.

Repeat with the next batch, with the remaining dried chilli and curry leaves, and serve hot with some lemon wedges.

500g (1lb 2oz) mussels
½ tsp salt, or to taste
6g (1 rounded tsp) finely grated root ginger (peeled weight)
4 large garlic cloves, finely grated
¾ tsp ground fennel seeds, or to taste
½ tsp freshly ground black pepper, or to taste
1 tsp ground cumin, or to taste
¼–½ tsp chilli (chili) powder, or to taste
3 tbsp vegetable oil
3½–4 tbsp rice flour (I often grind rice if I don't have any in)
2 tbsp semolina (optional)
2 dried chillies (chiles)
12 fresh curry leaves
lemon wedges, to serve

The tandoor oven cooks some of the most flavourful dishes in India, but is often skewed towards meat eaters. One of the few concessions to the large vegetarian population is tandoori cauliflower. I have to say, I love cauliflower, and this recipe gives it that extra edge. It is now a go-to appetizer for when I have friends round and don't want to serve a lot of meat or fish. It doesn't need a chutney or anything else. **Serves 6–8**

Tandoori cauliflower, my way

Cut the cauliflower into large 7.5cm (3in) florets. Bring a pot of water to the boil, add 1 tsp salt and the cauliflower. When it returns to the boil, cook for 1 minute, then drain.

Dry-roast the chickpea flour in a frying pan, stirring very often, until it has darkened by a couple of shades and smells roasted. Take it off the heat.

Place the cashews, garlic, ginger, oil and half the yogurt in a measuring jug or blender and blend until smooth. Stir in the remaining yogurt, spices, a little more salt and the chickpea flour. It should taste good, so adjust the salt if necessary. Place in a large bowl, add the cauliflower and leave for 20 minutes or so, if you have some time.

Preheat the oven to 200°C/400°F/gas mark 6. Line the base of the oven with foil, then oil an oven rack and place it in the middle of the oven. Once hot, place the cauliflower florets on the oiled rack and bake for 20–25 minutes, or until charred in areas and cooked through (the stalk should be tender when pierced with the point of a knife).

Meanwhile, mix together the coriander, tomatoes, chaat masala and chilli, then taste and adjust the seasoning. Spread the crème fraîche in a swirl over a serving platter. Spoon on just over half of the tomato mix. Place the cauliflower evenly over the crème fraîche, spoon over the rest of the tomato mix and serve.

For the cauliflower
900g (2lb) cauliflower (around 1 small one)
salt and freshly ground black pepper
4 tbsp chickpea (gram) flour
60g (½ cup) cashew nuts
3 small garlic cloves
20g (1½ tbsp) finely grated root ginger (peeled weight)
3 tbsp vegetable oil, plus more for the oven rack
400g (1¾ cups) plain yogurt
⅛–¼ tsp chilli (chili) powder, or to taste
paprika, for colour, if you like
1 tsp carom seeds
3 tsp garam masala (fresh if possible, see page 113)
3 tsp ground cumin

To serve
large handful of chopped coriander (cilantro)
2 small tomatoes, deseeded and chopped
¾ tsp chaat masala, or to taste
1 small Indian green finger chilli (chile), finely chopped, or to taste
200g (1 cup) crème fraîche

These are similar to fish cakes, but so much tastier. They speak of Goa's history: they are based on Portuguese meatballs but, as one of Goa's finest ingredients is seafood, it didn't take long for them to morph into prawn cakes. Goans love music, dance and meeting up with friends and – with a history of Portuguese rule and lots of elegant dining – Goan food soon had lots of appetizers. This is one of my favourites, the kind of thing you will eat in a Goan home rather than a restaurant. Serve them as they are with some lemon wedges, or with Tangy Herb Chutney (see page 182). **Makes 18**

Mini Goan prawn and coconut cakes

Put the coconut in a small cup, cover with hot water and leave to soak while you get on with the cooking.

Pound the cloves, black peppercorns, cumin and cinnamon until fine.

Heat 1½ tbsp oil in a large non-stick frying pan. Add the onion and fry until lightly golden on the edges. Add the ginger, garlic and some salt and cook for 45–60 seconds or until the garlic is cooked through. Add the prawns, turmeric and pounded spices and cook for 2 minutes, or until the prawns are just cooked through.

Scrape into a blender (or I use a hand-held blender). Drain the coconut, squeeze out the excess water and add to the prawns. Pulse-blend until much of the mixture is a rough mash, but still with some small pieces of prawns inside. Taste and adjust the seasoning. Stir in 2 tbsp each of the beaten egg and breadcrumbs along with the coriander and chilli. Allow to cool, then form into 18 equal patties. Place the remaining egg in a bowl, and the remaining breadcrumbs in a bowl.

Heat half the remaining oil in a large non-stick frying pan. Taking one cake at a time, dip in the egg and then coat well in the crumbs. Add half the cakes to the pan and fry until golden on both sides. Place on some kitchen paper to blot off excess oil, then repeat to cook the remaining patties. Serve hot.

3 good tbsp desiccated coconut
4 cloves
8 black peppercorns
1½ tsp cumin seeds
1cm (½in) cinnamon stick or cassia bark
3–4 tbsp vegetable oil
½ small onion, finely chopped
8g (1½ tsp) finely grated root ginger (peeled weight)
4 garlic cloves, finely grated
salt
350g (12oz) raw shelled prawns (shrimp), deveined
⅓ tsp ground turmeric
2 eggs, lightly beaten
45–50g (½ cup) dried breadcrumbs
large handful of coriander (cilantro) leaves, finely chopped
1 small Indian green finger chilli (chile), finely chopped

My mother was one of six sisters... and one brother. "Maasi" is the Hindi word for mum's sister. I have always loved my mother's extended family in Delhi: they are a group of resilient and independent women and most of my cousins from that side of the family are also women, all strong and lovely. My mother was the youngest sister. She grew up eating vegetarian meals often made without onions or garlic, yet the food was still so delicious and I always loved eating at my cousin's homes. One of my mother's sisters lived in the heart of Delhi; she was an amazing cook and would often cook for me and send food in a tiffin to the hotel when I was in the city. When I got interested in cooking Indian food, this maasi was the first person I turned to. This is one of the recipes I learned from her and I love it. I make big batches, half-fry them and freeze them for when friends come over. **Makes 10**

Maasi's lentil kichori

Wash the lentils and set them to soak for 30 minutes.

Put the plain flour in a bowl with a good pinch of salt. Mix in 2 tbsp oil with your fingers so the flour looks like sand. Knead in enough water to make a medium-firm dough, 80–90ml (⅓–generous ⅓ cup). Cover with a wet dish towel.

Dry-roast the chickpea flour in a non-stick saucepan over a low-ish heat, stirring almost constantly, until it darkens to a sandy colour and releases a distinctive aroma, 1–2 minutes. Set aside.

Clean the pan and heat 2 tbsp of the oil. Add the asafoetida and fry for 5–10 seconds or until it just colours. Add the cumin seeds and cook until sizzling and coloured. Add some salt, the ground coriander, garam masala, turmeric and chilli powder, stir for another 20 seconds or so, then tip in the drained lentils and season well. Stir well to mix and sauté for a few minutes or until all the liquid has dried up and the lentils have had a chance to cook in the spiced oil. Add a good splash of water, bring to a simmer, cover and cook until just tender, 8–10 minutes, or less if you soaked the lentils for a longer time. Dry off any excess water over a high heat; you want the mixture to be a bit moist and the lentils to have a little bite. Add the remaining ingredients, taste and adjust the seasoning. Set aside to cool. Divide into 10 portions.

Heat up 7.5–10cm (3–4in) of oil in a karahi, wok or saucepan until medium hot. Taking 1 ball of dough at a time, roll it out into a thin circle about 10cm (4in) wide. Fill with 1 rounded tbsp of the filling and enclose by pulling up the sides and making a pouch. As you pinch them to close the top, twist off the excess dough and set aside. Pat into a 1cm (½in) thick patty, making sure there are no holes on the top. Repeat to form another 4 and add all 5 to the oil. Immediately reduce the heat to low and fry really gently until golden brown and crispy on both sides, around 10 minutes. Repeat to form and cook the remaining balls, using the dough set aside from each to create any extras.

Serve hot with Tangy Herb Chutney, or Proper Date and Tamarind Chutney (pages 182 and 181).

100g (½ cup) yellow lentils (mung dal)
175g (1⅓ cups) plain (all-purpose) flour
salt
vegetable oil, as needed
1 tbsp chickpea (gram) flour
very small pinch of asafoetida
1 tsp cumin seeds
1½ tsp ground coriander
½–¾ tsp garam masala (fresh if possible, see page 113)
¼ tsp ground turmeric
⅛ tsp chilli (chili) powder, or to taste
½ tsp ground fennel seeds
½ tsp dried mango powder (amchur)
1 tbsp chopped coriander (cilantro)
2 tbsp thinly sliced spring onions (scallions, optional, but I like it)

Kathi rolls are hot Indian wraps and one of India's favourite streetfoods. They come in many guises, few of which resemble cold wraps as we know them. I have probably tried most versions, buying them in bustling markets in New Delhi, exchanging money straight from the car window in Mumbai – where they are known as Frankies – and in hotels and homes as streetfood made its way off the street. Different places have their own versions and there are no strict rules: as long as a soft bread with a slight chew envelopes a fresh, hot, tangy filling with red onions for crunch, you are in the right zone and in for a treat.

I make these often. They're tasty, everyone loves them and they are easy to throw together. You can also substitute chicken for the paneer. If you are in a hurry, you can buy tortilla wraps and cut them in half, but homemade wraps are cheaper and tastier. **Makes 10 medium-small, or 15 tiny, rolls**

Mini paneer kathi rolls

Blend together all the ingredients for the marinade. Season to taste with salt; I use 1 tsp. Add the paneer, gently turn the pieces to coat, and leave to marinate as you prepare the dough.

Put the flour in a bowl and pour in the oil, water and a good pinch of salt. Knead together well; it will be a bit squelchy at the beginning but should become lovely and soft without cracks once it is done. Cover with a damp dish towel and leave to rest for 20 minutes.

To make the breads, place a tava or frying pan over a medium heat. Divide the dough into 10 pieces and roll each out on a work surface lightly dusted with flour into a thin, round bread around 13cm (5in) in diameter. Dust any excess flour off the bread and place on the pan. Cook, turning once, until the bread has just a few light brown spots on both sides; it only takes a minute or so. Repeat to cook all the breads, stacking them on a dish towel, covering each with the corners as you go to help keep them soft. (You can also reheat them in some foil in the oven.)

Now back to the rolls. Heat the 2 tbsp oil in a saucepan, add the pepper and stir-fry for 2 minutes. Add the paneer and all its marinade and cook, stirring often, until the liquid has reduced and you can see oil in the pan, 6–8 minutes or so. You might need to add a splash of water at some point once the pan gets dry. Add the onions and cook for another minute, or until the liquid now just coats the ingredients and is still moist. Take off the heat.

Working quickly, spoon a line of the filling down the centre of each wrap, top with 1 rounded tsp Tangy Herb Chutney, wrap them up and serve hot.

For the marinade
100g (⅔ cup) plain yogurt,
  not too sour
20g (1½ tbsp) roughly chopped
  root ginger (peeled weight)
2 large garlic cloves
scant ⅔ tsp garam masala (fresh if
  possible, see page 113)
scant ⅔ tsp ground cumin
1 tsp chaat masala
½ tsp ground turmeric
2 tsp concentrated tomato purée
salt
⅛ tsp chilli (chili) powder,
  or to taste

For the rolls
240g (8¾oz) paneer, cut into small
  fingers 2cm (¾in) wide x 5cm
  (2in) long
2 tbsp vegetable oil
¾ small green (bell) pepper,
  thinly sliced
good handful of thinly sliced
  red onion rings
50ml (3½ tbsp) Tangy Herb
  Chutney (see page 182)
freshly ground black pepper

For the wrap
125g (1 cup) plain (all-purpose)
  flour, plus more to dust
1 tbsp vegetable oil
6–8 tbsp water, or as needed

Pani puri is one of my favourite streetfoods. It consists of a spherical crispy puri, often filled with potatoes and chickpeas, or sprouts, and topped with a flavoured water, or "pani". The "water" is spicy, salty, herby, sour and a little sweet. When I make them at home, I am always reinventing them as I come up with a new idea. I have kept this one quite close to the original, but have replaced the potato with avocado – as I think the creaminess works really well – and have added pomegranate seeds. Don't try to bite into these – they need to be placed whole in the mouth so they can explode into a delicious, complex bite-full. For special occasions, I often add ½ tsp crème fraîche on the top of the filling, before pouring in the pani; everyone prefers it this way, but it is optional. **Makes 35–40**

Sprouted lentil and pomegranate pani puris

Blend together all the ingredients for the pani; it is nice if you can still see little shreds of the leaves. Taste and adjust as necessary. It should be a little sour, sweet, salty, herby and spicy. Adjust the seasoning if necessary.

Bring a pot of salted water to the boil. Add the sprouts and return to the boil, then drain. When the sprouts are cool, mix them with the remaining filling ingredients. Salt lightly to taste.

When you are ready to serve, make medium-sized holes in the top of all the puris; through the side that is slightly thinner and easier to break gently. Pour the pani into a jug.

When you are ready to eat, either spoon 2 tsp of the filling into each puri and serve with the pani jug for people to serve themselves, or have the filling in a little bowl, so people can spoon and pour just before eating. I really love to dab a little sour cream on top of the filling before adding the spiced water.

For the pani
40g (2 packed cups) coriander (cilantro) leaves and stalks
20g (1 packed cup) mint leaves
6g (1 rounded tsp) roughly chopped root ginger (peeled weight)
3½ tbsp chaat masala, or to taste
5 tbsp tamarind chutney, or to taste (for homemade, see page 181)
600ml (2½ cups) filtered water

For the filling
salt
100g (3½oz) mixed sprouts, or mung bean sprouts
½ small red onion, finely chopped
½–⅔ large avocado, finely chopped
large handful of chopped coriander (cilantro)
¼ tsp roast and ground cumin seeds (see page 184)
seeds from ½ pomegranate

For the puris, and to serve
40 pani puris
sour cream, to serve (optional)

Papri and puris

These are both little crispy discs of pastry that are used in many Indian streetfood dishes and provide endless opportunity for culinary experimentation and sensory pleasure.

Papri is normally flattish and used in different layered chaats, most commonly with potatoes, chickpeas (garbanzo beans), yogurt, tamarind and coriander chutneys, or broken up to provide crunch in a bhel puri or other streetfood favourite. But they also make fantastic bite-size crispy vehicles for any variety of toppings (see page 12).

A **puri** is a three-dimensional spherical version of papri, but with slightly thinner pastry. It is delicate and, once you break open the upper surface, you can fill it with any combination of dry-ish ingredients (though wetter components will quickly soften the wafer-thin pastry) and then top it with a liquid. You immediately pop it into your mouth and the whole thing explodes into a taste and textural sensation! Again, while there are traditional fillings, feel free to explore other bits to add inside. I have a lot of fun adding new and unexpected ingredients to my puris, or to the water each is topped with, which add a fantastic element of surprise and fun to each mouthful (see page 48).

We have a lot of different ways of filling these crispy little discs that don't involve the flavoured water "pani". As it is streetfood, the authentic ingredients are generally inexpensive, but these little puris lend themselves to all sorts of fun in the kitchen and can make really pretty casings for a variety of more precious ingredients. This crab version is so delicious, if completely untraditional. **Makes 10 (can be doubled)**

Crab puris

For the puris
3 tbsp finely chopped tomato
2 tbsp finely chopped red onion, plus more to serve
good handful of chopped coriander (cilantro),
   plus more to serve
1 tsp finely chopped deseeded green chilli (chile)
½ avocado, finely chopped
50g (1¾oz) picked white crab meat
1½–2 tbsp lemon juice, or to taste
salt and freshly ground black pepper
10 pani puris

For the topping (optional)
3 tbsp light mayonnaise
1½ tsp tamarind paste

Mix together the tomato, onion, coriander, chilli, avocado, crab and most of the lemon juice and season to taste, adding extra lemon juice if you like.

Mix together the mayonnaise, tamarind, a little more salt and a few tbsp of water; the mixture should be creamy and not thick. Taste and adjust the seasoning.

When you are ready to serve, make medium-sized holes in the top of all the puris; through the side that is slightly thinner and easier to break gently. Spoon in a rounded tsp of the crab filling, top with the mayonnaise and sprinkle with coriander and red onion.

These are proper melt-in-your-Moghul-mouth kebabs. My mother lived with her sister-in-law after she got married. My mother came from a vegetarian family, but my father was a big meat eater, so she quickly learned some dishes from her sister-in-law who had grown up in Lucknow, a city famed for its refined dishes. More than anything, they love their red meat. This particular meat dish is made in the way they would cook them in the best restaurants in Lucknow. We serve them with drinks before dinner. You can make them a day in advance and refrigerate – or even freeze – them, then return them to room temperature and fry once your guests have arrived. If you think your blender won't manage to grind the whole spices once they are in the meat mixture, put them in a spice grinder first and add them to the meat already ground. **Makes 15 small kebabs**

Shammi lamb kebabs

Wash the chana dal and leave them to soak while you get organized.

Heat the 1 tbsp oil in a saucepan, add the onion and cook until well browned. Drain the oil into a bowl and add the lamb to the onion in the pan. Stir-fry until brown, then add the ginger, garlic, whole spices, bay leaves, salt and soaked lentils. Give the pan a good stir and add enough water to come three-quarters of the way up the lamb. Bring to the boil, then cover and simmer gently for 30–35 minutes, or until the lamb and lentils are soft.

Uncover and cook off any excess liquid over a high heat, stirring often so nothing burns. There should be no moisture left in the pan. Drain off any excess oil into the same bowl as that from frying the onions. Leave to cool for 10 minutes.

Place the meat mixture in a blender and blend until completely smooth; it may take a few minutes.

Stir in the green chilli, egg white, crumbs and coriander. Leave for another 10 minutes, or until cold.

Form into patties and leave to sit for a little longer if they are still soft.

Add 1–2 tbsp of the reserved oil into a large non-stick frying pan over a low heat and add as many kebabs as you can comfortably fit in. Carefully flip them once the underside is golden brown and cook this side in the same way.

Repeat with the next batch if you couldn't fit them all in. Serve hot with Tangy Herb Chutney or Minted Yogurt Chutney (see page 182).

4 tbsp chana dal
1 tbsp vegetable oil, plus
   1–2 tbsp more, if needed
1 onion, sliced
450g (1lb) minced (ground) lamb
15g (1 tbsp) roughly chopped root
   ginger (peeled weight)
4 large garlic cloves, roughly
   chopped
7 cloves
½ tsp black peppercorns
5mm (¼in) cinnamon stick or
   cassia bark
2 mace blades
4 black cardamom pods
3 dried bay leaves
salt, to taste (around ¾ tsp)
1–2 tsp finely chopped green chilli
   (chile), or to taste
1 egg white
1 large slice of bread, whizzed into
   crumbs
handful of chopped coriander
   (cilantro)

Kebabs are a huge favourite throughout India; you will find them everywhere and in many guises. This murgh hariyali version is deep and flavourful, with the herbs adding an amazing freshness. We serve these pretty little bites with drinks before dinner, with a little tangle of seasoned red onion slices drizzled with lemon juice and some Tangy Herb Chutney (see page 182). Typically, the little chunks would be taken off the skewers, but you can also cut the chicken into strips and serve them on small skewers; they look dramatic in little shot glasses with some chutney spooned into the bottom. These kebabs also work really well on the barbecue when a hot, sunny day beckons you outdoors, or they make delicious wraps with chutney and sour cream. Basically, they can work at almost any occasion. **Serves 4**

Herby grilled chicken tikka

Soak the bamboo skewers in water, to stop them catching when you cook the kebabs.

Blend together all the ingredients for the marinade until smooth. Taste and adjust the seasoning; it should taste slightly salty at this point. Add the chicken, cover and marinate in the fridge for at least 2–3 hours, or overnight is best.

Heat a fan-assisted grill (broiler) to a high heat, around 230°C/450°F/gas mark 8. Thread pieces of the chicken on to the skewers, keeping them close together to stop them drying out. Rest each end of the skewers across a deep roasting pan so that the meat is suspended in mid air.

Position the tray 5–7.5cm (2–3in) under the grill. Cook for 5–7 minutes, or until the chicken is lightly ch... rotate the skewers and cook for another 2–3 ... the meat start to brown, baste with melted bu... 30–40 seconds.

Remove the skewers from the heat and cool ... sliding the chunks off the skewers on to a pl... masala and serve with rings of red onions m... lemon juice, wedges of lemon and/or some ... (see page 182).

For the marinade

40g (2 packed cups) coriander (cilantro) stalks and leaves, torn a little

20g (1 packed cup) mint leaves

1 small Indian green finger chilli (chile), stalk removed, deseeded (optional)

15g (1 tbsp) roughly chopped root ginger (peeled weight)

6 large garlic cloves

... ground cumin

... riander

... sala (fresh if ... 113)

... thick

... e

... und black

... less boneless

... breasts, cut into

... s or long, thick

a little unsalted butter, melted

chaat masala, to serve

Black salt and chaat masala

I love discovering new tastes and useful ingredients that I can incorporate into my cooking and I think both of these ingredients would fall into that category for many people, especially for those readers who don't have roots in the Indian subcontinent themselves.

Black salt is a volcanic rock salt from the Himalayas, and found around some salt lakes in India. It has been used for hundreds of years in South East Asian cooking. It is salty, but also contains other compounds which give it more flavour than regular salt and, specifically, a sulphuric "eggy" smell. As you can imagine, the taste is quite unique and those who love it, *love* it. I would encourage you to be brave and give it a go. It is only used in small quantities, mostly in Indian streetfood, some chutneys, and yogurt dishes.

Chaat masala is one of my favourite spice blends. It is tangy from dried mango powder (amchur), spicy, salty and slightly sulphuric from the inclusion of black salt (see above). It is an important component of one of India's favourite types of streetfood: chaat. Chaat is hard to describe in a single sentence, but can be anything from a simple tossed salad with a chaat masala spice blend (see page 30), to more complex layered dishes with chutneys and yogurt. Chaat loosely means "to lick one's fingers", and Indians feel this way about these types of dishes. I have never made my own chaat masala as the storebought jars are really good, so I always, always have some in the larder. I add it to lots of streetfood, but also sprinkle it over simple grilled foods that need a bit of flavour. It is one of the most useful and well-used spice blends in my kitchen.

Samosas were one of the first things I learned to cook, at about ten years old. My mother would sit me down at the kitchen table with homemade fillings and storebought pastry strips and I would try my hardest to form perfect triangular samosas. These would be fried up when guests came and I eagerly collected compliments for my efforts. While we made mini cocktail samosas for drinks, they are normally served as a teatime snack with a cup of masala tea where they are b???? and the pastry is shorter. This is a samosa with homemade crumbly pastry an? ??? ?????? would be in those street stalls back in India. All you need is a cup ?? ??? ??? ???? ??? ind Chutney or Tangy Herb Chutney (see pages 181 an? ??

Proper punj??

To make the dough, place the fl??? ??? ??? ??? ?????? ?????? ?pastry
tsp salt and drizzle over 2 tbsp o? ??? ??? ??? ??? ?? cup) plain (all-purpose)
until it resembles fine sand and c??? ??? ???
the dough will be a little wet, but ??? ??? ???
become a medium-soft dough. Co??? ??? ?????getable oil, or ghee, or
leave to rest as you make the filling ??? ??? ??s more vegetable oil to
??? ??ry
For the filling, heat the remaining 3 ??? ??? ???½ tbsp water
over a medium heat. Add the cumin ??? ???
until coloured and aromatic. Add th??? ??? ?????oft. Add **For the filling**
the ginger and cook for another minu??, ???n tip in the potatoes and   ⅔ tsp cumin seeds
some salt, cover and cook over a medium-low heat until the potatoes   ⅔ tsp coriander seeds
are soft, stirring every so often; it will take around 10 minutes.   ½ medium-small onion, finely
                                                                           chopped
Now add the peas, chilli and ground spices and cook for another   ¾ tsp finely chopped root ginger
minute or so, mashing the mixture with the back of a spoon. You   350g (12oz) potatoes, peeled and
should see lots of potatoes and peas, but it should be held together   cut into small cubes
with the mashed bits. Stir in the coriander. Taste and adjust the salt 1 good handful of frozen peas
and spice as necessary. Leave to cool.   1 tsp chopped green chilli (chile),
                                                                           or to taste
Take a large, deep saucepan or karahi and fill with 15–18cm (6–7in)   ¼ tsp chilli (chili) powder, or to
oil. Heat gently as you make the samosas.   taste
                                                                       ⅔ tsp ground turmeric, or to taste
To make the samosas, make 20 equal balls out of the dough. Roll out   ⅔ tsp ground cumin, or to taste
each ball into an oval or round, around 5mm (¼in) thick. Cut this in   1 tsp dried mango powder
half widthways. Spread a little water along the flat edge and – taking   (amchur), or to taste
the piece in your hands – bring it together, folding one side of the   1½ tsp ground coriander, or to taste
straight edge to make a triangular pocket, sealing well. These are a   ⅓ tsp garam masala (fresh if
little fiddly when small, so remember they don't have to be perfect.   possible, see page 113), or to taste
Now place the pocket in your cupped hand and fill with the stuffing. large handful of chopped coriander
Rub water on the open edge and seal to form a triangular samosa.   (cilantro)

Once you have formed 10 samosas and the oil is nice and hot,
add them to the oil. Fry over a medium heat until golden all over,
5–7 minutes. Repeat to form and fry the rest.

Serve hot with chutneys.

Uttapams are like pizzas, but lightly pan-fried and traditionally made from a batter of rice and lentils that is lightly fermented to give a certain sourness. The whole authentic process takes more than a day, so instead I often use this mixture of semolina and a little rice flour mixed with yogurt for sourness. It makes a light snack to serve to friends, or even to children as a meal. I have given two options for the topping below, so take your pick, as both are delicious. You can make these earlier in the day or the day before, and reheat them in a dry frying pan when you're ready to eat. **Makes 10 small uttapam (can be doubled)**

Mini semolina tamil "pizzas"

Mix the semolina and rice flour with the yogurt and 120ml (½ cup) water and set aside for 1 hour.

After 1 hour, add the cumin, onion, ginger, pepper, tomato, chilli, dried curry leaves (if using) and salt. You should have a batter that can hold its shape but isn't not too thick. If that is not the case, stir in a little more water.

Place a medium-large non-stick frying pan over a medium-low heat and add 1 tbsp of the oil. When it is hot, add 1 tbsp batter for each uttapam, in heaps. Add around 5 of these. Cook over a low-ish heat until the underside is golden and crisp. Meanwhile, scatter over the shredded fresh curry leaves (if using). Flip over and cook this "presentation" side only until it has light golden spots in places. Place on kitchen paper to blot off excess oil and repeat with the rest of the batter and oil.

Serve hot with your choice of topping, see below.

For a crème fraîche and tomato topping

Add a good pinch of brown mustard seeds to a little hot vegetable oil. Once they are popping, add 8 curry leaves. Follow 30 seconds later with ½ finely sliced red onion. Cook over a high heat, stirring often, until the edges darken. Add 2 small finely chopped tomatoes and continue cooking over a high heat, stirring, until the tomatoes soften and release some juices into the pan. Season and take off the heat. Serve the uttapams with a quenelle of crème fraîche, topped with a small spoon of the tomato mixture.

For a traditional chutney topping

Top each uttapam with 1 rounded tsp Coconut Chutney and sprinkle over some Dry Garlic Chutney (see page 180).

90g (½ cup) fine or medium grain semolina

2 tbsp rice flour (optional, but makes them crispier)

70g (generous ¼ cup) plain yogurt, ideally sour (if yours isn't, use a little more)

⅓ tsp cumin seeds

½ small red onion, finely chopped

2 tsp finely chopped root ginger

2 tbsp finely chopped red (bell) pepper

½ tomato, finely chopped

½–1 small Indian green finger chilli (chile), thinly sliced

15 dried curry leaves, roughly crushed, or 10 fresh curry leaves, shredded

½ rounded tsp salt

2 tbsp vegetable oil

Indian summer

Strictly speaking, Indians don't eat outside in the summer; the sun is too hot, the temperatures soar, and there are monsoons to take into consideration. However, they do love to eat al fresco where possible and, when the weather cools, people try to spend time outdoors. I have memories of sitting on a roof terrace on a woven rope day bed taking tea with thick Indian savoury biscuits (*matthi*); or eating lunch in cool shaded gardens, or on the fan-cooled verandahs of the old-world clubs that still exist in the country. There are many Indian evening festivities spent outdoors, wrapping yourself in a shawl as it cools… and, of course, a multitude of weddings (mine included) which are held entirely outside.

Back in the UK, when the sun shone, my family would light the barbecue, although our staples were a bit different from others. There were no burgers, buns or hot dogs; instead we ate tandoori-style chicken drumsticks, spiced lamb chops and skewers of meat, all marinated overnight so, by the time we ate them, they had lots of flavour. These were served with toasted pitta bread (naan wasn't widely available yet) and a salad, while hummus and taramasalata were served with them instead of traditional chutneys. It worked; we loved it all and we loved it together.

India doesn't have a barbecue culture as such, but there are many street-side grills making amazing skewered kebabs, while a host of others have mastered cooking in the coal-fired tandoor ovens that are in almost all Indian restaurants. Add to this the many delicious traditional marinades and the resulting meats are both very moist and truly flavourful. Also, India's large vegetarian population have ensured this style of eating includes paneer and fresh vegetables, coated in lighter, sympathetic flavours but equally delicious. There are also vegetables cooked on large braziers on street carts: sweetcorn, sweet potatoes and other local produce that works well over a grill.

All of the dishes in this chapter are inspired by food I have eaten in India on the street or in a restaurant but – while most are traditional – some are based on streetfood memories, which I use as a stepping stone to create more Westernized vegetarian barbecue dishes. There is so much to inspire and borrow from Indian food that it is hard to stop at so few.

Tandoori chicken is my all-time favourite dish to order in an Indian restaurant. Flavourful, light, moist and delicious, all I need with it is some Minted Yogurt Chutney, crisp red onions marinated in seasoned lemon juice and Naan (see pages 182 and 197). Most people love tandoori chicken, especially when made with some kind of charcoal which adds its delicious smokiness to the flavours. This is a truly delicious way to eat chicken, whether it is sunny or not. There are no tricks except a long marinating time (and not over-cooking the chicken!) so that the flavours can seep deep into the flesh and the chicken becomes really juicy. I have used Kashmiri chilli powder to get some of that intense red colour in my chicken as opposed to food colouring, but you can leave it all out and just eat it without the red colour. The flavours speak for themselves. **Makes 8 pieces (can be doubled)**

Tandoori-style chicken

Slash each piece of chicken 3 times down to the bone at the thickest parts of the flesh. Place in a bowl and marinate in about half the lemon juice and half the salt for 30 minutes if possible.

Blend together all the ingredients for the marinade (except the lemon wedges) until smooth (add the extra lemon and salt if you didn't marinate it as above). Add to the chicken and leave to marinate for as long as possible – preferably overnight, covered in the fridge – but at least for 3–4 hours.

Remove the chicken from the fridge 30 minutes or so before cooking. Preheat the barbecue to a medium-high heat, or preheat your oven grill (broiler) to a fan-assisted high setting and line a baking sheet with foil.

Place the chicken on the barbecue and cook, turning often and moving around to prevent burning and hot spots, until charred and cooked through, 20–22 minutes, turning often. Or place the chicken on the prepared baking sheet under the grill, and grill until charred on both sides and cooked through; it should take the same amount of time. If it is cooked but not very brown, move closer to the grill bars for a few minutes at the end of cooking time.

Baste with the butter – mixed with the paprika or Kashmiri chilli powder, if you like -- sprinkle over the chaat masala and ground fenugreek, and serve with lemon wedges and Minted Yogurt Chutney (see page 182).

For the chicken

8 skinless chicken thighs, legs, or both
a slice of unsalted butter, melted
a little paprika or Kashmiri chilli (chili) powder
1 tsp chaat masala
1 tsp ground fenugreek

For the marinade

2½ tbsp lemon juice, plus lemon wedges, to serve
1 rounded tsp salt
120g (½ cup) full-fat plain yogurt
4 large garlic cloves
1 Indian green finger chilli (chile), deseeded (optional)
15g (1 tbsp) roughly chopped root ginger (peeled weight)
1½–2 tsp Kashmiri chilli (chili) powder, or paprika (for colour)
1 rounded tsp ground cumin
1 rounded tsp garam masala (fresh if possible, see page 113)
2 tbsp vegetable oil

Indians cook a lot of kebabs, often highly spiced and flavoured from the inside so you need little with it. A burger, though, is quite different. The elements that go with the burger are almost as important as the meat itself to a perfect, sense-satisfying end. This burger has those qualities, the burger itself is lightly flavoured, the onions add sweetness, bite and a little flavoured crunch from the seeds, while the roasted chilli yogurt brings creamy, spicy moreishness which makes them hard to put down. A really great, grown-up burger, these will soon become a favourite. **Makes 5–6**

Best-ever burgers with spiced onions

Mix together all the ingredients for the burgers (except the buns and sliced tomato), season with 1¼–1½ tsp salt and leave to rest for 30 minutes.

You can either cook the chillies on the barbecue later, or do them in a frying or griddle pan in advance. Wherever you cook them, place them directly on the hot surface and cook, turning once the underside has charred and blistered. Once they are done, wrap in cling film (plastic wrap) and set aside.

Heat the oil for the onions in a frying pan and, once hot, add the panch phoran. Cook for 20–30 seconds, or until the seeds are popping and colouring. Add the onions and a good pinch of salt and cook over a high heat until they have coloured and are well browned on the edges, 5–7 minutes. Adjust the seasoning and set aside. (You can reheat these on the barbecue later in a flameproof pan, or keep them warm in a low oven.)

Mix together the yogurt, mayonnaise and coriander for the topping, adding a good grinding of black pepper and salt lightly. Once the chillies are cool, peel off their skins, slit lengthways and deseed; discard the seeds. Then chop the flesh up and add to the yogurt. Set aside.

When you are ready to barbecue, make 5–6 large patties out of the minced meat mixture, remembering to make a little flat indent in the centre lightly with your fingers; this will help them cook evenly and not puff up in the middle. Preheat the barbecue.

Place on the hottest part of the grill and cook for 4–5 minutes, or until a little crisp and charred, then turn over and cook for another 1–2 minutes. Place 1 slice of the tomato on the base of each bun, top with a burger, a generous dollop of the yogurt, which should start oozing with the heat, and some onions. Place on the lid and eat immediately.

For the burgers
450g (1lb) minced (ground) beef or lamb, with some fat on it
1 red onion, finely chopped
10g (2 tsp) finely chopped root ginger (peeled weight)
2 large garlic cloves, finely grated
¾ tsp garam masala (fresh if possible, see page 113)
1 egg
salt and freshly ground black pepper
5–6 burger buns or baps
1 large tomato, sliced crossways

For the roasted green chilli yogurt
3 large green chillies (chiles), stalks removed, pierced with the tip of a knife
2 rounded tbsp thick Greek yogurt
2 tbsp crème fraîche or mayonnaise
good handful of chopped coriander (cilantro)

For the spiced caramelized onions
1½ tbsp vegetable oil
½ tsp panch phoran
2 red onions, thinly sliced

Chillies

Chillies are native to Central and South America and research suggests they have been purposefully grown as food for more than 6,000 years. They were called "peppers" by Christopher Columbus, as their fieriness reminded him of the heat from the peppercorns that were familiar to him. Chillies were introduced to India in the 15th century; before that, Indians used a spice called "long pepper" for heat in their food.

Six hundred years later, India is now the world's largest producer and consumer of chillies… and sometimes it is hard to find an Indian meal that does not contain them. Different regions have their own varieties, and use more or less heat in their food, with the dishes of the South of India being the hottest.

Chillies are known to be addictive, so Indians should be forgiven for loving the hot, fiery fruits as much as they do! The sting on the tongue from eating chillies stimulates the pain receptors in the brain, which then release endorphins (the body's natural pain killers) into the body, making you feel good. Therefore, chillies = happiness! They are also full of vitamins C, E and A and beta-carotene and are powerful anti-inflammatories, even used medicinally in this respect.

Chillies add more than heat to a dish – they add flavour as well – especially green chillies, which have a lovely distinctive taste to offer along with their spiciness. The heat is mostly contained in the seeds and inner membranes, so I often leave a chilli whole to get the flavours without too much heat (pierce the chilli with a knife, though, otherwise it might burst while being fried).

Most Indian dishes will feel anaemic in both colour and flavour without the addition of chillies. They add an edge and dimension to the cuisine that is one of its greatest draws, and Indian food wouldn't quite be Indian food without them.

Tandoori fish is always a treat; the gentle tandoori flavour and the carom seeds here work so well with fish. I cook this on the barbecue in those hinged grills for whole fish. The result is smoky, tangy and lightly spicy. I use Kashmiri chilli powder as it has a mild heat but a vibrant colour, which somehow whets the appetite when you are eating tandoori-style dishes. These are deceptively easy to make once you are confident with a barbecue. You can also make this in the oven: I force a couple of skewers along the length of the body and place them on the edges of the baking tray so that the fish is cooked suspended, as in a proper tandoori oven. You can also make little fish tikkas with this recipe, using good firm fish pieces, under a hot grill. Serve with Tangy Herb Chutney (see page 182) and a crunchy salad. **Serves 4**

Barbecued tandoori-style sea bream

Using a sharp knife, score each fish 4 times on each side through the skin, about 5mm (¼in) into the flesh. Squeeze over some lemon juice and sprinkle a little salt inside and out, then set aside for 10–15 minutes.

Blend together all the ingredients for the marinade except the carom seeds and chickpea flour. I often add a little extra paprika for a good red colour. Taste and adjust the seasoning; at this stage it should taste a bit too salty and spicy, and that's fine. Add the carom seeds and chickpea flour.

Smear the marinade thickly over both sides of each fish and into the slits. Leave to marinate for 45–60 minutes.

Meanwhile, preheat the barbecue to a medium-high flame. I like to use a hinged fish rack in which I put the fish, but be careful that it doesn't flatten it too much. (You can also use 2 metal skewers per fish.) Oil the grill rack and the fish rack.

Place the fish on the heat and cook for 6–8 minutes on the first side, or until the underside is a lovely golden colour with some areas of charring. If the coals are too hot, rake them away slightly. Turn the fish and cook the underside in the same way. If using skewers, the fish might stick a little, so be careful before turning. The fish is done when golden on both sides; to check if it is done on the inside, you can use a thermometer which should read 60°C (140°F) when poked into the thickest part of the fish.

Baste both sides with the melted butter as it cooks and chars, adding paprika to the butter for a good colour, if you want. Sprinkle with chaat masala and serve with lemon or lime wedges and coriander.

For the fish
2 whole sea bream, or snapper, cleaned, gutted, scaled and fins removed by the fishmonger
a few squeezes of lemon juice, plus lemon wedges, to serve, or lime wedges
salt
a little vegetable oil
1–2 tbsp unsalted butter, melted, to baste
a little paprika (optional)
a few good pinches of chaat masala
coriander (cilantro), to serve

For the marinade
4 large garlic cloves
10g (2 tsp) roughly chopped root ginger (peeled weight)
3 tsp lemon juice
1–2 tsp Kashmiri chilli (chili) powder, or paprika for colour and chilli powder for heat
1 tsp ground cumin
2 tbsp vegetable oil
150g (½ cup) plain yogurt
¼ tsp freshly ground black pepper
½ tsp carom seeds
1 rounded tbsp chickpea (gram) flour

Paneer is such a big part of Punjabi cuisine that no proper Punjabi menu can be written without it. You eat it at home as a vegetarian main course, on the streets as a battered pakora with tea or a quick meal of scrambled spiced paneer served with a bun. In restaurants, they cook tandoori paneer to cater for vegetarian clients. Here, I cook the paneer in a parcel on top of the barbecue, adding so much of the herby green marinade that it is almost a sauce. It is really simple to make and really delicious. Cook the paneer over indirect heat, or with the cover on your barbecue, so it has time to heat all the way through. I like to finish it off over the high heat to get a little charring on the base, through the foil. **Serves 4–6 (can be halved)**

Grilled herby paneer parcel

Place the paneer in a bowl of boiling salted water for 10–15 minutes to soften.

Meanwhile, wash the herbs really well, including the coriander stalks. Squeeze lightly to get rid of the excess water. Place in a good food processor or blender with the ginger, garlic, lemon juice, oil, yogurt, ground spices and 1 rounded tsp salt. Whizz until quite fine and smooth. Stir in the cream and carom seeds, if using. Taste and adjust any spices or seasoning to taste.

Prepare a parcel with enough foil to make a generous double or triple layer around the block of paneer. Place a good coating of the marinade in the middle of the parcel, place the paneer on top and coat well with the remaining marinade. Cover loosely and leave to marinate for as long as possible, putting it in the fridge if longer than 1 hour.

When ready to cook, preheat the barbecue.

Scatter the onion and green chilli over the parcel. Bring the foil together to make a parcel that encompasses the cheese completely. Place straight over indirect heat on the hot grill, or place the cover on your barbecue if you have one, and cook for 8–10 minutes or until the paneer has heated right through and is steamy; ideally you should see a little charring coming through at the bottom. Finish off over a high heat.

Serve the paneer in the foil, or place on a plate and sprinkle over a little extra chaat masala and serve hot, I like to leave a knife next to it so people can cut their own slices.

For the paneer
450g (1lb) block of paneer, (if fresh, make with 1.8 litres/5 pints of whole milk, see page 147)
salt
2 tbsp finely chopped red onion
1 Indian green finger chilli (chile), thinly sliced

For the green herb paste
70g (3½ packed cups) coriander (cilantro) leaves and stalks
25g (1 generous packed cup) mint leaves
12g (1 scant tbsp) roughly chopped root ginger (peeled weight)
2 large garlic cloves
4 tsp lemon juice
1 tbsp vegetable oil
4 tbsp thick Greek yogurt
1 tsp chaat masala, plus more to serve, or to taste
1 tsp garam masala (fresh if possible, see page 113), or to taste
1 tsp ground cumin, or to taste
2 tbsp double (heavy) cream
½ tsp carom seeds, if you have some

North India grows lovely sweet potatoes, they are white-fleshed, sweet and creamy. When in season, they are grilled whole in their skins on street stalls and served with lemon juice and the delicious spice blend chaat masala, that balances out their inherent sweetness. This is a Westernized, embellished version of that dish, made with orange-fleshed sweet potatoes. It works really, really well. It is a fusion dish but one that, for me, works better than both originals and makes an amazing summery salad. **Serves 4–6 as a side dish**

Charred, spiced sweet potato salad

Cut the potatoes into large wedges: the best way is to halve them horizontally and wedge each side. Place in a large pot of boiling salted water, return to the boil and simmer until the tip of a knife goes through easily, 8–10 minutes.

Meanwhile, make the dressing. Whisk together the lemon juice, mayonnaise, yogurt, half the oil, the chaat masala and garlic; season to taste. Heat the remaining olive oil in a small saucepan, tilting it so the oil collects in one area. When hot, add the mustard seeds and reduce the heat. After 5 seconds, follow with the fennel seeds and cook until the mustard seeds pop, another few seconds or so. Stir into the dressing and season to taste.

Drain the cooked potatoes and, once dry, place on a hot oiled griddle and cook for 1–2 minutes on each side, or until the wedges have lovely grill stripes. Add them straight into the dressing with the red onion, green chilli and most of the pumpkins seeds and leaves. Toss well, garnish with the remaining seeds and leaves and serve.

For the sweet potatoes
2 large sweet potatoes (around 450g/1lb in total), scrubbed
salt and lots of freshly ground black pepper
a little vegetable oil
¼ small red onion, very thinly sliced
1 Indian green finger chilli (chile), deseeded and finely chopped
1 tbsp pumpkin seeds, lightly toasted in a pan until puffed up
2 large handfuls of watercress or rocket (arugula)

For the dressing
2 tsp lemon juice
4 tbsp mayonnaise, low-fat if you like
2 rounded tbsp Greek yogurt
2 tbsp extra virgin olive oil
½–¾ tsp chaat masala
1 medium-small garlic clove, finely grated
½ tsp brown mustard seeds
½ tsp fennel seeds

The Bengalis have a delicious dish of little aubergine rounds nestling in a lightly creamy mustard and yogurt sauce. It is truly tasty and forms the inspiration for this barbecue dish. Here I make the sauce separately (and very quickly), adding some tomatoes to the basic recipe, and have swapped the aubergines for courgettes, which work so well with the mustard flavours. This is an amazing side dish for any barbecue, but also makes a lovely, light course for vegetarians, in which case I sometimes add ricotta and/or two large handfuls of chickpeas for protein. A Bengali would use mustard seeds but, when you grind mustard seeds, they can sometimes turn bitter, so unless you are already familiar with this delicious but fickle spice, use the prepared mustard as I do here. It works just as well, you just lose a little extra body. The sauce is also delicious with some barbecued chicken and fish, so maybe make extra! **Serves 2–3**

Barbecued courgettes with Bengali sauce

If using mustard seeds, soak them in 60ml (4 tbsp) water for 15 minutes. Add a large pinch of salt, the ginger and garlic and blend until smooth. The mustard seeds do not need to break down completely. It will smell lovely and mustardy.

If using prepared mustard, blend the ginger and garlic with some water and mix with the mustard and some salt.

Heat the oil in a small non-stick pan. Add the panch phoran and, as the seeds pop, reduce the heat, add the green chillies and fry for another 10 seconds.

Add the mustard seed paste (if using), cleaning the blender container with a little water and adding it to the pot. Cook for a few minutes or until the garlic smells cooked and has darkened ever so slightly. Add the yogurt, most of the tomato, salt and turmeric and stir continuously until it comes to the boil. Stir in the prepared mustard (if using) and a splash of water and return to the boil, it should have the consistency of light cream. Adjust the mustard and salt to taste: it should be punchy, the vegetable can take it. Set aside.

Preheat the barbecue to medium-hot.

Brush the courgette slices with olive oil, place on the grill rack and cook, until charred on both sides, around 2 minutes each side. Meanwhile, place the mustard sauce in a flameproof pan on the barbecue as well, to reheat the sauce, or just reheat it on the hob.

Place the courgettes on your serving plate, top with the ricotta, then the sauce, reserved tomato, coriander and pumpkin seeds. Serve hot.

3 tsp prepared English mustard, or 2 tsp brown mustard seeds (see introduction above), or to taste
salt
10g (2 tsp) roughly chopped root ginger (peeled weight)
3 large garlic cloves, halved
3½ tbsp extra virgin olive oil, plus more to brush the courgettes
½ tsp panch phoran
3–4 Indian green finger chillies (chiles), stalks removed, pierced with the tip of a knife
3 quite rounded tbsp thick Greek yogurt
1 large tomato, chopped
½ tsp ground turmeric
3 courgettes (zucchini), sliced diagonally into 1.5cm (⅝in) thick rounds
150g (⅔ cup) ricotta
handful of chopped coriander (cilantro)
2½ tbsp pumpkin seeds, lightly toasted in a pan until puffed up

This is a really popular way of cooking fish in Kerala. They use a whole flat fish, which they slash to the bone on either side. I have used a butterflied fish here, but you can also use 2 fillets sandwiched together. The banana leaf adds a flavour and smokiness. You can buy banana leaves in some Asian stores, but not all, so check before you make a trip. You can also cook these in foil. This is a mild tomato-based dish with those typical Keralan flavours that work so well with fish. You can make this up earlier in the day and then just barbecue it to heat through. You can also cook these on a griddle pan. **Serves 2–4**

Keralan banana leaf-wrapped fish

Mix together all the marinade ingredients. Season well and add ½ tsp black pepper to it. Add the fish (if using whole fish, slash it deeply on each side first) and leave to marinate for 30–60 minutes.

Now make the masala paste. Heat the coconut oil in a non-stick frying pan. Add the mustard and cumin seeds, once they start to pop, add the onion and ginger, green chillies, curry leaves and some seasoning and cook until the onions have softened. Add the garlic and cook for another minute or until the onions are browning a little. Add the ground spices, tomatoes and a splash of water and cook over a high-ish flame until the masala releases oil into the pan, around 10 minutes. It should look like a paste. Taste and adjust the seasoning, adding a good grinding of black pepper. Scrape into a bowl and set aside. Give the pan a wipe.

Now add the remaining 1 tbsp of oil into the pan, add the fish, skin side down, and cook over a medium-high heat until crisp and lightly brown, around 1 minute, then turn over and cook for another 30–40 seconds on this side.

When you are ready to eat, smear ¼ of the masala on a banana leaf, place the fish on top and top with a similar amount of the paste. Repeat with the other fish. Enclose each fish, envelope style, in a leaf, there should be enough leaf wrapped around to keep it secure, but you can also secure the parcels with some wet twine or toothpicks.

When you are ready to cook, preheat the barbecue. Place the banana leaf parcels on the barbecue rack and cook for 2–3 minutes on each side if cooking from room temperature, or closer to 5 minutes on each side if cooking from chilled. If you are using whole fish, it will take longer to cook. The banana leaf will char in places. Serve with some lime wedges.

For the marinade
½ tsp ground turmeric
1 rounded tsp finely grated root
  ginger
1 rounded tsp finely grated garlic
1½ tbsp lemon juice
salt and freshly ground black
  pepper

For the fish
2 small sea bream, cleaned and
  butterflied, or 4 sea bream fillets,
  or even whole fish, if you prefer
1 tbsp coconut or vegetable oil
1 large banana leaf, tough stalk
  removed, cut into large rectangles
  (heat on the hob to make it pliable)
lime wedges, to serve

For the masala paste
1 tbsp coconut or vegetable oil
¼ tsp brown mustard seeds
¼ tsp cumin seeds
1 small red onion, finely chopped
1¼ tbsp finely chopped root ginger
2–4 green chillies (chiles), stalks
  removed, pierced with a knife
10 fresh curry leaves
4 large garlic cloves, finely chopped
¼–½ tsp chilli (chili) powder
¼ tsp ground turmeric
1½ tsp ground coriander
¾ tsp ground cumin
½ tsp ground fennel seed
2 medium-small tomatoes, chopped

Rajasthani royalty were known to hunt often, hosting hunt parties in their countryside lodges. In those days, the gains were marinated and cooked over charcoal, or in a large pit. They were known for using a lot of yogurt and chillies in their dishes, but not too much complex spicing. These venison kebabs are typical of those dishes: the flavours are really harmonious, not too tart as with some other meaty kebabs, not too spicy and very moreish. The smokiness is a big part of the flavour so, even when this is cooked indoors in a Rajasthani kitchen, it is often smoked with some hot coals, a little ghee and cloves. These are great kebabs and a natural to cook on the BBQ, and you can also make them with chicken, lamb or beef. I bought a pack of venison pieces pre-cut for a stir-fry and used them in this dish. They are thin enough to flash cook, but not too thin that they dry out. These flavours really lift this lean meat. **Serves 4**

Rajasthani smoky venison kebabs

Heat 2.5cm (1in) of oil in a small pan. Add the onion and fry until brown. When you take them out, they should crisp up. Pour the oil into a bowl, leaving behind 1 tsp in the pan. Add the garlic and cook until just colouring at the edges.

Pour this into a blender with the onion and remaining marinade ingredients, adding 2 tbsp of the onion oil. Blend until smooth, adding 1 tbsp or so of water to help the blades turn. Taste and adjust the chilli and salt, then stir in the caraway seeds. Add the venison pieces and marinate for a few hours if possible – or at least 1 hour – to allow the flavours to penetrate. Soak the skewers for 30 minutes, so they don't catch and burn on the barbecue.

When you are ready to cook, preheat the barbecue and return the meat to room temperature if you have put it in the fridge.

Skewer the venison pieces on the soaked bamboo skewers, or use thin metal ones. Place on the grill rack and cook for 4–6 minutes, turning halfway. Then baste with the ghee or butter and cook for another 30 seconds on each side. Serve with the lemon wedges, some Minted Yogurt Chutney (see page 182) and some onion rings.

For the kebabs
½ tsp caraway seeds
250g (9oz) venison pieces
bamboo skewers
25g (2 tbsp) ghee or unsalted butter, melted, to baste
lemon wedges, to serve

For the marinade
vegetable oil
1 onion, thinly sliced (or 45g /1½oz bought crisp fried brown onions)
5 large garlic cloves, sliced
150g (½ cup) Greek yogurt
15g (1 tbsp) roughly chopped root ginger (peeled weight)
2 tsp garam masala (fresh if possible, see page 113)
½ tsp chilli (chili) powder, or to taste
3–4 tsp lemon juice
1 good tsp salt, or to taste

Garam masala

Garam masala literally means "hot spices" and refers to India's most famous spice blend. A garam masala will vary from region to region – and even from one home to the next – with family recipes closely guarded… though the spice mix itself will be happily distributed to those who need it.

The most popular blend – and perhaps the most complex – is the typical Punjabi version, which uses the largest variety of spices (though, as a Punjabi, perhaps I would say that, wouldn't I…!). A typical blend contains black peppercorns, cloves, cumin, cinnamon, black and green cardamom pods, dried Indian bay leaves and – sometimes – mace and nutmeg.

As a typical Punjabi, I do not dry-roast the spices to make them nutty – I feel that can cause the volatile oils to be released too early and disappear, and also that the roasted flavour can be a bit overpowering to simple ingredients – but I do sometimes very lightly toast all the spices together in a large pan, just so they grind easily and finely.

Storebought garam masala just doesn't have the same flavour as homemade, and a dish made with it will simply never be as good as one made with fresh spices. If you love flavour, please put aside 10 minutes to make your own batch (see page 113) and – if you don't want a lot of spices lurking around in the cupboard afterwards – make it a big one that you can share with friends. It is the Indian way… and also makes you the best kind of friend.

Corn on the cob was either boiled and served with butter at home, or grilled on the bustling streets of India until charred and blistered, and served with a spice blend and lemon. My father still only eats the Indian version, so we grill it over the flame of the gas cooker and turn until charred. For the buttered type, brush the cobs with butter or crème fraîche, then add the spices; this lends tang and creaminess. **Serves 4**

Flame-grilled spiced sweetcorn

4 sweetcorn cobs
2 tbsp chaat masala
⅛–¼ tsp chilli (chili) powder, or to taste
a little unsalted butter or low-fat crème fraîche (optional, see introduction above)
1 lemon, cut lengthways into 4–6 wedges

Peel back the husks of the sweetcorn, leaving them attached to the cobs. Remove the silky bits and wash the cobs well. Mix the chaat masala and chilli powder in a small bowl.

Preheat the barbecue. Grill the sweetcorn directly over a high heat, turning often with the leaves, until lightly charred all over (if it rains you can do this directly over a gas flame). When cooked, smear each cob with butter or crème fraîche, if you want.

Serve the sweetcorn with the lemon wedges and a little mound of the spice blend on the side. Dip the wedge in the spices and rub them over the sweetcorn, squeezing a little lemon juice on as you do, and serve.

My husband recently came back from a trip to India, raving about a mustard-flavoured tandoori broccoli dish that he had at his hotel – sarsonwali broccoli... and it reminded me how much I like this strong but delicious tandoori flavour. I love mustard in all its guises but if you don't feel the same way, use another oil and add some mustard powder to the marinade, or leave the mustard out all together. It will still taste lovely. **Serves 4**

Mustard grilled broccoli

225g (8oz) broccoli, cut into 5cm (2in) florets
salt
1½ tsp chickpea (gram) flour
2 large garlic cloves, finely grated
15g (1 tbsp) finely grated root ginger (peeled weight)
2 tbsp mustard oil
3 tsp lemon juice
2 rounded tbsp thick Greek yogurt
½ tsp ground cumin
vegetable oil, for the barbecue

Quickly blanch the broccoli in salted water, then refresh in cold water, drain and set aside.

Dry-roast the chickpea flour in a frying pan, stirring it all the time until it darkens by a couple of shades and smells roasted. Stir it with remaining ingredients (not the oil) and ¾ tsp salt. Taste and adjust the seasoning. Pour straight into a large bowl.

Shake the excess water off the broccoli and add to the marinade, then toss well to coat.

Preheat the barbecue. Oil the rack and place the broccoli on top, then cook for 6–7 minutes, turning the vegetable over until it is lightly charred in places. (Alternatively, cook under the grill [broiler] in your oven. Preheat the grill to high, place the broccoli on the upper middle shelf and cook until charred, turning to cook the underside as well.)

Serve hot.

Coastal curries

The Indian coastline is about 7,500km (4,660 miles) long, and the food changes as you travel south down the west coast to the very tip of India – a place called Kanyakumari – where the three main bodies of water surrounding India meet: the Arabian Sea, the Indian Ocean and the Bay of Bengal. It changes again as you move back up the east coast. While the main ingredients are the same, India's food scene has seen numerous influences rippling in from the coast over the last millennia, as different colonizers and traders visited and settled on her shores.

My first memory of the Indian coastline is of a broad, beautiful Goan beach on a family holiday, when I was around 12. All I really remember is the beach, playing cards with family friends and the beach-side grilled seafood… which was amazing. I didn't return until about four years ago, this time with my own children, for a family holiday. My husband isn't adventurous with food and wasn't keen on trying the local fare but compromised – after a bit of nagging – and I booked somewhere known for authentic Goan food. As we walked in, I double-checked (as always) that the kitchen could make something without any chillies for the children, but, as with many restaurants catering to locals, the spice bases were already made. My husband and children happily trooped off to eat elsewhere while I stayed and enjoyed my first proper Goan meal in my own company, focusing entirely on the food: best decision of the holiday!

The quality and variety of Indian seafood are truly amazing, and fishermen along the coast have been spicing their wares with dexterity and care for centuries, choosing spices that enhance rather than encroach upon the delicate flavours. The resulting dishes are just delicious, the seafood lending its flavour to the sauce and the spices returning the favour to the fish; working as a beautiful whole. Different regions have their own ways of using spices, with distinct and exciting results.

But Indian coastal food is more than seafood. I have been to sea-facing Ayurvedic spas in Kerala where the food is healthy, light, and completely vegetarian. I've eaten in Calicut, where Moplah food uses the same coastal ingredients, but in much meatier ways. The food in Tamil Nadu is known for its crisp rice and lentil pancakes (*dosas*) and brothy, spicy lentil stews (*sambhars*), all eaten with fresh coconut chutney. Indian coastal food is defined as much by its seasonings as by its fresh ingredients and, in the case of this chapter, coconuts, curry leaves, mustard seeds, fresh black pepper (on the west coast), red chillies and tamarind are all defining flavour profiles. So this chapter has something for everyone; the only criteria is that every dish could feature on a menu by the Indian sea.

This reminds me why I love the dishes of Kerala so much. There are so many different cooking techniques and styles, as all the three main religions of India are reflected in Keralan food, and an abundance of delicious fish, chicken, lamb, beef, duck, lentils and vegetable dishes. There are loads of delicious beef dishes in Kerala, but this is my favourite. It is rich and meaty, but the lovely distinct flavours of Kerala definitely shine out, in particular the curry leaves, coconut, fennel seeds and black pepper. This is a typical Christian dish and one they might cook on special occasions although, apart from grinding your own spice blend, it is quite straightforward. Fortunately, as coconut and coconut oil are so in fashion these days, it has become really easy to find them both, so no more fiddling with large unyielding coconuts. Yay! This is so delicious, you just can't stop eating it, nugget after nugget. **Serves 6–8**

Malayali beef with coconut slivers

Grind together all the spices for the spice blend until fine.

Heat a large saucepan or casserole with the oil and add the beef, onions, garlic, ginger, salt, vinegar, turmeric, green chillies, coconut, curry leaves and the spice blend. Sauté for 6–8 minutes, then add a good splash of water, bring to the boil, cover and simmer gently until the beef is tender, around 70–80 minutes (or this can be less or more depending on the heat level, so do check). Keep giving the pot a stir and make sure there is enough water in the pan, but try not to add too much.

When the meat is soft, make the temper. Heat the oil in a large sauté pan or saucepan. Add the mustard seeds and, as they are sizzling, add the curry leaves and red chillies. Follow 10 seconds later with the onions and some salt. Sauté for 7–8 minutes or until the onion has lovely golden edges and smells caramelized. Add the julienned ginger, stir for 20 seconds, then tip in the beef and all its juices. This is the time that you "fry" the meat. Cook it over a medium heat until it has darkened a bit and the moisture just coats the beef, 10–15 minutes.

Taste, adjust the seasoning and serve.

For the spice blend
1 tbsp fennel seeds
1½ tsp cumin seeds
2 tsp black peppercorns
1½ tbsp coriander seeds
5 cloves
seeds from 3 green cardamom pods
2.5cm (1in) cinnamon stick

For the beef
4 tbsp coconut oil
800g (1lb 12oz) braising beef pieces
2 onions, thinly sliced
5 garlic cloves, finely grated
40g (3 tbsp) finely grated root ginger
  (peeled weight)
salt
2 capfuls of white wine vinegar
¾ tsp ground turmeric
1–3 green chillies (chiles), stalks
  removed, pierced with a knife
70g (¾ cup) fresh coconut slivers
small handful of fresh or dried
  curry leaves

For the tempering
5 tbsp coconut oil
1 tsp mustard seeds
small handful of fresh or dried
  curry leaves
2 dried chillies (chiles)
1 medium-small onion, thinly sliced
10g (1 rounded tbsp) finely julienned
  root ginger (cut from a long piece)

Kolhapuri dishes are known to be spicy but deeply flavourful. Their spice blends are softer and more fragrant than garam masala and – once you have a jar – you don't really need a lot of other spices. The blend here does have a fair number of ingredients in it, but it takes under 5 minutes to do from beginning to end, will keep well for future use and goes with chicken, meat, and even some meaty vegetables. If you are missing a couple of the ingredients, don't worry, it will still be fine. If you have some good-quality garam masala, you can even leave out the first 7 ingredients (these are all in my Garam Masala, see page 113). I make this dish with mutton, which adds more flavour than lamb, but you can use lamb instead. The flavours are incredible whichever meat you use. Serve with Indian breads or Simple, Perfect Rice (see page 189). **Serves 4**

Kolhapuri mutton curry

Set a wok or small frying pan over a medium-low heat. Pour in the first six ingredients for the masala and stir-fry over a low heat for 20 seconds. Add the coriander, cumin, fennel and fenugreek seeds and continue until they are toasted too, another 1–2 minutes. Pour straight into your spice grinder. Then add the poppy and sesame seeds and the coconut and dry-roast until golden. Add to the other spices and grind until it is all a fine powder. Store in an airtight container. This will keep for a month or more, in a dark, airtight place.

Blend together the ginger, garlic, the quartered onion, the 25g of coriander, salt, chilli, 3 tbsp of the Kohlapuri masala and the turmeric until smooth. Add a little water if necessary to help the blades turn. Add to the meat and marinate for as long as possible, ideally overnight in the fridge, but you can continue without as well.

Heat the oil in a large pan over a medium heat. Sauté the sliced onions with a little salt until well coloured on the edges; I like to do this over high-ish heat. Add the meat with its marinade along with the tomatoes. Bring to the boil, then cover, and cook until all the water has dried up, around 45 minutes over a medium heat. Keep giving the pot the occasional stir.

Now increase the heat and stir-fry the meat in the thickened masala paste, to help intensify the flavours, for 3–4 minutes. Stir in another 3½ tbsp of the Kohlapuri masala and enough water to cover the meat. Return to the boil and cook gently until the meat is soft, anything from another 15–20 minutes for lamb, and a little longer for mutton. Splash in some more water if necessary as it cooks down.

Once done, taste and adjust the seasoning, adding more heat (chilli powder) and the remaining Kohlapuri masala, if you like. I like this dish with a little sauce to mop up with my bread, so add enough boiling water accordingly, or you can keep it as a drier curry. Serve sprinkled with coriander.

For the Kohlapuri masala (makes 10–11 tbsp in total)

3 cloves
1 star anise
2 dried bay leaves
½ tsp black peppercorns
1cm (½in) cinnamon stick
2–3 dried chillies (chiles, optional)
1 tbsp coriander seeds
2 tsp cumin seeds
2 tsp fennel seeds
small pinch of fenugreek seeds
1 rounded tbsp poppy seeds
1 rounded tbsp sesame seeds
4 tbsp desiccated coconut

For the curry

20g (1½ tbsp) root ginger (peeled weight), roughly chopped
8 large garlic cloves
2 onions: ½ quartered, 1½ thinly sliced
25g (1 cup) coriander (cilantro), plus a good handful to serve
¾ tsp salt
1 tsp Kashmiri chilli (chili) powder (optional, for colour)
7–8 tbsp Kohlapuri Masala (see above), or to taste
1 tsp ground turmeric
700g (1lb 9oz) diced mutton or lamb, with some bones if possible
4–5 tbsp vegetable oil
2 large tomatoes, roughly chopped

Kerala is a beautiful, verdant coastal region and its food is as abundant as the waters of the Arabian sea that laps it. If you look at Kerala on the Indian map, it looks like a languishing green chilli along the coast and I find a similar sense of serenity in the people. When you visit Kerala, it does seem as though time slows down, whether you are on a houseboat, slowly gliding along the backwater canals, stopping for a bite to eat at one of the restaurants bordering the canals, or staying in one of the many Ayurvedic spas. It is full of character, but it isn't brash. This fish curry is a little like that, full of delicious coastal flavours (fish, curry leaves, coconut), even green chillies and other spices, but with nothing harsh about it. It is comforting enough for every day, but elegant enough to serve to friends. Serve with Simple, Perfect Rice, or Tamil-style Lemon Rice (see pages 189 and 192). **Serves 4**

Fish pappas

Marinate the fish with all the remaining ingredients in the list and 2 good pinches of salt and leave for 20 minutes or so.

Heat the 5 tbsp oil in a large non-stick saucepan. Add the mustard and fenugreek seeds. Once the popping slows down, add the curry leaves. Follow within 10 seconds with the onions and some salt. Cook until soft and just turning colour. Add the ginger and stir-fry for 30 seconds.

As the onions cook, blend the tomato and garlic until smooth. Add to the ginger along with the powdered spices and a splash of water. Cook until the paste releases oil back into the pan, a good 8–10 minutes or so. Then stir-fry the paste for another couple of minutes. Taste: the garlic should be cooked and it should taste harmonious and a bit salty at this stage.

Add the coconut milk and chillies, bring to the boil, cover and cook for 4–5 minutes. Meanwhile, heat the remaining 2 tbsp oil in a large, non-stick frying pan and add the fish; you might have to do this in 2 batches. Fry over a medium-high heat until lightly golden on both sides. Place on a plate and repeat with the second batch. It shouldn't take more than 2–3 minutes in total for each batch.

Add 350ml (1½ cups) water to the sauce pot, along with the vinegar, and bring to the boil. Cook for 4–5 minutes. Taste and add more salt if necessary. Add the fish and coconut cream to the pot and cook for 3–5 minutes more, turning the pieces of fish halfway through. The fish should be cooked and the sauce should be creamy.

For the marinade

600g (1lb 5oz) halibut, cut into large pieces (I quarter steaks)
½ tsp ground turmeric
1 large garlic clove, finely grated
10g (2 tsp) grated root ginger, juice squeezed out (discard the fibres)
2 tsp lemon juice
1 tsp vegetable oil
salt and ground black pepper

For the sauce

5 tbsp coconut or vegetable oil, plus 2 tbsp for the fish
⅔ tsp brown mustard seeds
⅓ tsp fenugreek seeds
15 curry leaves, fresh if possible
2 onions, finely chopped
30g (2 tbsp) finely chopped or grated root ginger (peeled weight)
1 large tomato
45g (10–11 large) garlic cloves
⅔ tsp ground turmeric
2 tsp ground coriander
1½ tsp ground fennel seeds
¼ tsp chilli (chili) powder
1 tsp garam masala (see page 113)
400ml (14oz) can of coconut milk
4–6 small Indian green chillies (chiles), stalks removed, pricked with a knife
1½–2 tbsp white wine or other vinegar
50g (3 generous tbsp) coconut cream

Mangalorean food is so delicious, yet still undiscovered on this side of the world. I was introduced to it at the house of a friend, who had a Mangalorean lady coming to cook for her on occasion. She made a fish curry and it was just so delicious, it got me curious. I had some more Mangalorean food in restaurants in Bombay, but it was only when I got married that I found out more about it. The lady who was co-ordinating the marriage for the hotel was Mangalorean and, over the time it took to plan the wedding, I had learned a lot more. She also gave me a cookbook one of her relatives had written, to help me to understand it properly. I have since fallen in love with the food of this region... I haven't tried a bad dish yet. I have simplified this recipe to appeal to busy cooks. Serve with Simple, Perfect Rice or Skinny Rice Dosas (see pages 189 and 193). **Serves 4**

Mangalorean prawn ghassi

Wash the prawns well, apply a little salt and turmeric, and set aside.

Heat 1 tsp of the oil in a small pan and gently roast the coriander seeds, fenugreek seeds, cumin seeds, black peppercorns and dried chillies. Once they have darkened a little and are aromatic, scrape straight into a spice grinder and grind to a fine powder.

Place the spice powder into a blender with the coconut, the quartered onion, garlic, ginger, the ½ tsp ground turmeric, the tamarind and enough water to help the blades turn, and blend until very smooth; it might take a few minutes to get it smooth, but persevere.

Heat the remaining oil in a non-stick pan, add the chopped onion and some salt and sauté until coloured on the edges. Add the paste and sauté for 10–12 minutes or until it releases oil back into the pan; it will stick so do keep an eye on it and stir as necessary. Then stir-fry for another 4–5 minutes or so over a high-ish flame until it moves around in a ball around the pan. Taste, it should be harmonious. Add chilli powder to taste, if required.

Add 480ml (2 cups) water and stir well as you bring it to the boil, then reduce the heat a little and simmer for 2–3 minutes. Add the prawns, cover and cook over a medium heat until the prawns are done, just 2–3 minutes. Taste, adjust the seasoning and the level of tang with tamarind and serve hot.

500g (1lb 2oz) raw prawns (shrimp), shelled and deveined, but tails left on
salt
½ tsp ground turmeric, plus more for the prawns
3–4 tbsp vegetable or coconut oil
1 rounded tbsp coriander seeds
good pinch of fenugreek seeds
1 tsp cumin seeds
15 black peppercorns
3–6 dried Kashmiri chillies (chiles, less hot than normal dried chillies), or 2–4 regular dried chillies
115g (1¼ cups) grated fresh coconut (find it fresh in many supermarkets, or frozen in Asian stores)
2 onions, 1 quartered, 1 finely chopped
5 large garlic cloves
20g (1½ tbsp) roughly chopped root ginger (peeled weight)
chilli (chili) powder, to taste (optional)
2½ tbsp tamarind paste, or to taste

A second Mangalorean dish in one chapter is testament to how much I enjoy the food from this city, located in the state of Karnataka on the west coast of India. It is considered one of the cleanest and least polluted parts of the country. It has always been an important strategic port on the Malabar coast, fought over and passed between different rulers for the last 500 years. The region has always been an exporter of spices, chillies and cashew nuts. A glimpse at the food and you can see an abundance of all those elements. This is probably one of their most famous dishes – rich with roasted spice, coconut sauce and just the right amount of tang from tamarind. In Mangalore it is eaten with the crisp flakes of a thin bread made of rice paste. Alternatively, serve with Skinny Rice Dosas (also a Mangalorean rice bread), Simple, Perfect Rice, Flaky Malabar Paratha (pages 193, 189 and 195), or plain parathas. **Serves 4–6**

Mangalorean chicken curry

Start with the spice blend. In a non-stick frying pan over a low heat, dry-roast all the whole spices and chillies until aromatic and turning colour, 1–2 minutes. Pour into a spice grinder and grind until fine. Add the coconut to the pan and dry-roast over a medium heat until golden. Pour into a blender.

Now for the curry. Heat 1 tbsp of the ghee or oil in the pan over a high heat and fry the sliced onion with some salt until coloured on the edges. Add to the coconut with the ground spices, the garlic, ginger and a splash of water and blend until really smooth.

Heat 2 more tbsp ghee or oil in a large non-stick saucepan over a medium-high heat and add 1 of the chopped onions with some salt; cook until soft, then add the chicken. Sear on all sides, then add the spice blend and a splash more water. Bring to the boil, then cover and cook for 25 minutes, stirring occasionally and making sure the pan has not run dry (add a splash more water if it does).

Towards the end of this time, heat up the remaining 1 tbsp ghee or oil in the frying pan and add the curry leaves and the 2 extra dried chillies. Cook for 30 seconds, then add the final onion and cook until well browned.

Meanwhile, add most of the coconut milk and most of the tamarind to the chicken and stir well, then bring to the boil. Add the contents of the tarka pan and stir well. Taste and adjust the seasoning and the tamarind; add some chilli powder if you would like more heat, or a little more coconut milk if you find it too hot.

For the spice blend
2 tbsp coriander seeds
1½ tsp cumin seeds
½ tsp black peppercorns
3 cloves
2.5cm (1in) cinnamon stick
  or cassia bark
2–4 dried chillies (chiles), plus
  2 more for the tarka
140g (5oz) fresh or frozen coconut,
  grated
10 large garlic cloves
10g (2 tsp) finely chopped root
  ginger (peeled weight)

For the curry
4 tbsp ghee or vegetable oil
3 small onions, 1 sliced, 2 finely
  chopped
salt
1kg (2lb 4oz) skinless bone-in
  chicken joints, cut into medium
  pieces
16–18 fresh curry leaves
300ml (1¼ cups) coconut milk,
  or to taste
3–4 tsp tamarind paste
a little chilli (chili) powder,
  to taste (optional)

One of my father's cousins owned a chicken farm in Delhi and every few years we were invited for a big family reunion. We always asked our cousins to take us to see the chicks. They were fluffy, postcard-cute and perfect, running around in their large pen. I never asked what my uncle did with all these chicks and chickens; I just accepted it like I did our large, loud and interesting extended family. We always left with a basket of fresh eggs which would be eaten over the next few days as fried eggs on toast (sprinkled with salt and red chilli powder), or delicious egg curries. Since then I have always loved egg curry with rice, which is so much tastier than it sounds. There are many versions in India, but perhaps the most famous is this Malayali breakfast dish from Kerala, a tangle of browned onions, curry leaves, green chillies and tomatoes. Try them with a Skinny Rice Dosa (see page 193), or some buttered toast! **Serves 3–4**

Malayali egg roast

Heat a pan of hot water big enough to fit the eggs. Once it is boiling, add the eggs and boil for 10 minutes. Pour out the water and remove the eggs.

Meanwhile, heat the coconut oil and butter in a wide non-stick saucepan. Add the curry leaves and chillies and fry for 40 seconds. Add the onions and some salt and sauté until soft and colouring on the edges; this is important as this dish is characterized by the tangle of browned onions. Add the ginger and garlic and cook gently until the garlic smells cooked. Add the powdered spices and give them a few good stirs in the pan.

Now tip in the tomatoes and cook for 10–12 minutes or until soft, and the masala releases oil back into the pan.

Meanwhile, peel the eggs and halve lengthways, or cut a deep lengthways slit into each without going the whole way through.

Add 120ml (½ cup) water to the pot and return to the boil. Taste and adjust the seasoning, add the eggs, stir once, or shake the pan to bring it all together, cover and simmer for 4–5 minutes, then serve sprinkled with coriander.

6 eggs
3 tbsp coconut oil
1 tsp unsalted butter or ghee
12–14 fresh or dried curry leaves
2–3 Indian green finger chillies (chiles), stalks removed, pierced with a knife
2 red onions, thinly sliced
salt
12g (scant 1 tbsp) finely chopped root ginger (peeled weight)
3 large garlic cloves, finely chopped
⅔ tsp ground turmeric
1 tsp ground fennel seeds
1 tbsp ground coriander
¼ tsp freshly ground black pepper
¼ tsp chilli (chili) powder, or to taste
1 tsp garam masala (fresh if possible, see page 113)
2 tomatoes, sliced
handful of chopped coriander (cilantro), to serve

The last time I went to Goa, I was with my family and I am forever trying to get them all to try new flavours around India. But as Goa is best known for its seafood, my husband was very hesitant to try any local fare. I found a well-regarded restaurant and ordered lots of amazing Goan vegetarian food to try to convince them all. I have to be honest, I don't think I managed it, but I did discover loads of lovely vegetarian Goan dishes that I love and have decided to keep in my life. This caldine is a mild but flavourful curry and will not overpower the vegetables. **Serves 3–4**

Mushroom and bean caldine

Start with the caldine paste. Grind the coriander seeds, cumin, peppercorns and cloves to a fine powder. Place the tomato, the quartered half onion, garlic, ginger and turmeric in a blender and blend until smooth.

Heat the oil in a non-stick saucepan. Add the sliced onion and cook over a high-ish heat until caramelized and brown on the edges. Add the spice paste and a fair amount of salt and cook for 5 minutes or until the masala releases oil back into the pan. Add the mushrooms and stir-fry until they release water. Continue cooking until the masala is really thick, darkened and is sticking to the mushrooms.

Add the beans, chillies and a splash of water, cover and cook for another 4–5 minutes. Add the coconut cream with as much water as you want for a creamy curry. Bring to the boil, add the tamarind, season to taste and simmer for 2–3 minutes. Serve with the coriander.

For the caldine paste
2 tsp coriander seeds
1 rounded tsp cumin seeds
8 peppercorns
4 cloves
1 medium-large tomato
½ onion, quartered
5 large garlic cloves
15g (1 tbsp) roughly chopped
    root ginger (peeled weight)
½ tsp ground turmeric

For the dish
3 tbsp coconut or vegetable oil
½ onion, thinly sliced
salt
450g (1lb) brown chestnut
    mushrooms (shiitake or shimeji
    mushrooms are also great here),
    rinsed and halved
150g (1¼ cups) cooked cannellini
    beans
2–4 Indian green finger chillies
    (chiles), stalks removed, pierced
    with a knife
50–60g (about 2 tbsp) coconut
    cream, or to taste
1 tsp tamarind paste, or to taste
handful of coriander (cilantro),
    to serve

Having grown up with a father who absolutely loved good food (I'm sure most of our holidays were based around a city he wanted to eat at) and also had a general passion for travel and eating, I have had my fair share of the world's delicious crab dishes. I've eaten fried soft-shell crabs by the Potomac in Washington, crab cakes in New York, chilli crab in Singapore... and just American-style, cooked and served with a butter sauce. But, I have to say, none are quite as delicious as India's Malabar Coast crab dishes. Cooked with local spices and coconut, you are literally licking your fingers as you break bits open. Many feel that cooking an expensive crab with Indian spices is a waste and that the flavours would be drowned out. I think that cooking it any other way is a waste of good crab! This is not a watery curry; here the sauce is thick but not so dry it clings. **Serves 4**

Coastal crab and coconut curry

Heat the oil in a large non-stick karahi, wok or saucepan. Add the mustard seeds and, as they are popping, add the curry leaves and cook for another 10 seconds or so. Add the onion and a little salt and cook until it is soft and has a good golden brown colour on the edges, around 10 minutes.

Meanwhile, make a paste in a blender of the ginger and garlic with some water. Add to the pan and cook for 1–2 minutes or so, or until the water has dried off and the garlic smells cooked.

Add the tomatoes, seasoning and powdered spices and cook well until the masala releases oil into the pan, around 15 minutes, stirring often. Once it has released oil into the pan, stir-fry over a high heat to darken a little. This will deepen the flavour and colour.

Meanwhile, blend the coconut with some water until smooth. Once the tomatoes are done, add the coconut and chillies, bring back to the boil and add the crab. Cook for 2–3 minutes, then add enough water to come just halfway up the crab. Return to the boil, cover and simmer for 15 minutes.

Once the crab is done, add most of the tamarind, taste and adjust the seasoning and add more tamarind or chilli powder for more tang or heat respectively. There should be a lot of thick sauce; this is not a watery curry, you should be able to eat the creamy sauce with rice.

Serve sprinkled with coriander or coconut, or both.

5 tbsp vegetable oil
1 tsp brown mustard seeds
15 fresh or dried curry leaves
1 onion, finely chopped
salt
40g (2 rounded tbsp) roughly chopped root ginger (peeled weight)
cloves from ½ large head of garlic
400g (14oz/4 medium-large) tomatoes, blended until smooth
¼–½ tsp chilli (chili) powder, or to taste
½ tsp ground turmeric
2 tsp ground cumin
2 tsp ground coriander
¾ tsp freshly ground black pepper
3 tsp garam masala (fresh if possible, see page 113)
80g (¾ cup) fresh grated coconut (you can buy this frozen in Asian supermarkets as well as fresh in some supermarkets now), plus more to serve (optional)
2–3 green chillies (chiles), stalks removed, pierced with a knife
1 medium-sized crab, around 1.2kg (2lb 12oz) cleaned, lightly broken up in places
2 tsp tamarind paste, or to taste
handful of chopped coriander (cilantro, optional), to serve

A thoran is a simple Southern stir-fry with mustard seeds, curry leaves, shallots, cumin and fresh coconut. It is a typical vegetable side dish served in Kerala, especially on feast days as part of a banana leaf-laden offering. This is a fairly typical recipe, as beetroot is a local vegetable they love to cook in this way. I have added the chard as I love the texture and earthiness it brings to the dish, and it feels virtuous with it as well! You can vary this recipe with a host of other vegetables and greens and, in fact, they also make thorans from leftover red meat and chicken, so you can add some of that in as well. I also often add a can of chickpeas if I am serving this as a main course, as the earthiness and mealiness work really well with these flavours. It is also a lovely side dish to serve with a lentil curry, grilled meats or Tamil-style Lemon Rice (see page 192). **Serves 4–6**

Beetroot and ruby chard thoran

Heat the oil in a non-stick saucepan over a medium heat. Add the mustard seeds, lentils and dried chillies and reduce the heat. Once the popping of the mustard seeds starts to subside and the lentils have turned a light golden, add the curry leaves. Follow 5 seconds later with the chopped beetroot and some salt. Stir well for a few minutes, then reduce the heat.

Cover and cook for 18–20 minutes, or until beginning to soften (it depends on how large the beetroot was chopped).

Meanwhile, blend together the shallots or onion, coconut, cumin, ginger and garlic without any water. It will form a coarse paste.

Add the paste to the beetroot and cook gently for 5–6 minutes, stirring occasionally, then add the chard. Cook for another 3–4 minutes or until the whole thing is done. Taste and adjust the seasoning, sprinkle with the extra coconut and serve.

2 tbsp coconut oil
¾ tsp brown mustard seeds
2 tsp urad dal (split and skinned black lentils), if you have them
2–4 dried chillies (chiles)
20 fresh curry leaves
500g (1lb 2oz) raw beetroots (beets), peeled and chopped into 1cm (½in) cubes
salt
2 small shallots, or ½ red onion, quartered
80g (¾ cup) grated fresh coconut, plus more to serve
1 tsp cumin seeds
18g (1 rounded tbsp) finely chopped root ginger (peeled weight)
1 large garlic clove
14 large stems of ruby or rainbow chard, leaves shredded, tender stems sliced

This hails from West Bengal and although the state has a coast, much of its fish and seafood is from freshwater sources such as rivers and lakes. Fish and prawns are one of their most important sources of protein and are eaten in some form at least once a day. The other food love there is mustard – seeds, oil and paste. There is something magical about making your own mustard paste, watching the seeds transform into familiar yellow mustard with its strong, sharp smell. Until I went to Bengal, I had no idea how beautifully mustard worked with seafood, but the way the Bengalis make this and their fish curry (see page 162) shows they are masters of strong but restrained flavours. One last note: the Bengalis are the only peoples of India, as far as I know, who eat in courses, so often a dish comes out by itself. This dish stands up to being eaten alone, or with Simple, Perfect Rice (see page 189). **Serves 4**

Bengali stir-fried prawns with mustard

Rub the prawns with the ginger, garlic, turmeric and a good pinch of salt. Leave for 20 minutes.

Meanwhile, blend the mustard seeds with 2–3 tbsp water until fine (the husks of the seeds will still be there).

Heat the oil in a large frying pan. Add the onion and cook until soft and colouring at the edges. Add the green chillies and sauté for about 30–40 seconds. Now tip in the prawns and stir-fry for 30 seconds. Add 2½ tbsp of the mustard paste, a little splash of hot water, the chilli powder and coconut cream and sauté for another minute or so until the prawns are cooked.

Taste and adjust the seasoning. Stir in the chopped coriander and serve hot.

400g (14oz) large raw tiger prawns (jumbo shrimp), shelled and deveined, but tails left on
1½ tbsp finely grated root ginger
5 garlic cloves, finely grated
⅔ tsp ground turmeric
salt
1½ tbsp brown mustard seeds
2 tbsp vegetable or mustard oil
½ onion, finely chopped
2–3 green chillies (chiles), stalks removed, each pierced with a knife
¼ tsp chilli (chili) powder, or to taste
2 rounded tbsp coconut cream, or to taste
handful of chopped coriander (cilantro)

Chettinad is a community in the region of Tamil Nadu, on the southern tip of India, known for its delicious but spicy meaty dishes such as Southern Peppery Chettinad Chicken (see page 146). The same flavours work well with "meaty" vegetables, like in this aubergine dish. Vegetarian food in India has always been the best in the world and it is dishes like these which lead the way and make vegetables so exciting. **Serves 3–4 (can easily be doubled)**

Chettinad aubergine coconut curry

Heat ½ tsp of the oil in a large non-stick sauté pan that has a lid. Add the ingredients for the masala and gently roast for 45–60 seconds, or until the coriander seeds have coloured a little and smell roasted. Pour into a spice grinder or a good mortar and pestle and grind well until fine.

Dry-roast the coconut in the same pan until golden. Place in a container to blend, add the masala and a good splash of water and blend to a fine paste; this takes a few minutes. Set aside.

Separately, blend the tomato with the garlic and ginger until smooth.

Give the pan a wipe and heat the remaining oil. Add the mustard seeds and, once they are popping, add the curry leaves. After a beat add the onion and cook until well golden on the edges. Add the potatoes and cook for a minute and add the blended tomatoes and turmeric and a little more seasoning; cook over a moderate heat for 3–4 minutes or until the masala has darkened.

Now make a deep cross through the aubergines so they are cut into quarters lengthways but still held together at the stalk end. Add the aubergines, coconut paste, green chillies and a good splash of water to the pan and bring to the boil. Cover and cook gently for about 18–20 minutes or until the vegetables are soft. Give the pan the occasional stir and add a splash of hot water from the kettle when the masala begins to looks dry and is starting to stick. It should be a little thicker than double (heavy) cream when done.

Taste and adjust the seasoning if needed. Serve hot, sprinkled with the coriander.

For the Chettinad masala

1–2 dried red chillies (chiles), to taste (I use 1)
½ rounded tsp cumin seeds
1 rounded tsp coriander seeds
½ rounded tsp fennel seeds
8 black peppercorns
2 thumbnail-sized shards of cinnamon stick or cassia bark
10 fresh or dried curry leaves

For the curry

3 tbsp vegetable oil
4 tbsp grated fresh coconut or 2 rounded tbsp desiccated coconut
1 large tomato, chopped
3 garlic cloves
8g (1½ tsp) roughly chopped root ginger (peeled weight)
⅓ tsp brown mustard seeds
10 fresh or dried curry leaves
1 onion, finely chopped
1 potato, peeled and cut into 2.5cm (1in) pieces
½ tsp ground turmeric
200g (6–8) baby aubergines (eggplant)
1–2 green chillies (chiles), stalks removed, pierced with a knife
small handful of coriander (cilantro), to serve

Coconut

Coconuts are such an important ingredient for millions of Indians. They are part of the food culture wherever they grow, but have transcended the table: they are now considered important in industry, as coconut fibres have many useful applications, while the whole nut is used symbolically in many Hindu religious rituals.

In India, coconut flesh is loved and used in many ways. It might be blended into a fine paste, or the milk extracted from the flesh (the blended paste adds more texture; the milk and cream more sweetness). The flesh itself might be chopped, slivered or grated, sautéed into a stir-fry or fashioned into desserts. Coconut water is only ever drunk, never cooked with.

While the West is now researching the benefits of eating coconuts after their recent boom in popularity, Indian Ayurvedic medicine has been loving them for thousands of years… but believe that not all coconuts are created equal. Young green coconuts – which are around 90% water with moist, jelly-like, thin flesh – are considered good for cooling the body and helping to unclog blocked channels to help your body's own *prana* or *chi* (loosely translated as our "energy" and "life force") move freely. Once the coconut matures into middle age, the flesh is drier and fattier; it is thought to contain more nutrients, fat, carbohydrates and minerals, so this is the best stage at which to eat them. (A fully mature coconut is considered hard to digest and heavy on the system – especially if your digestive system isn't strong – and best avoided.) On the whole, though, coconuts are considered cooling and heavy, a fantastic nourishing ingredient, but not to be consumed in excess. (Cooking coconut with spices will help you digest it better and also warm up these cool tendencies.) Younger nuts are also considered to be very good for the skin and hair, joints, respiratory illness, strength and immunity.

A quick word on coconut oil. After being vilified for decades, it has emerged as a health hero, with many scientists saying it is the best oil to cook with as it is more heat-stable than many others. It is made up of medium-length fatty acid chains (most other oils have longer ones), which are easier to digest, so is good for weight management. On top of this, it is considered very good for cognitive health and the heart and is anti-microbial, so it's also good for immunity. The people from Kerala (incidentally, this region is named after the coconut) have always used coconut oil as their primary cooking medium, so cooking one of the Malayali (Keralan) dishes from this book is a great place to start getting healthy!

Thanks to this new appreciation, we now find coconut oil, water, snackable pieces and frozen grated coconut in supermarkets and Asian shops in the West. So, make like the Malayalis and crack open those coconuts!

On high days and holidays

There are so many religions in India and all religious holidays are officially celebrated. The main religion alone – Hinduism – has so many gods and festivals, and that adds up to around 130 holidays in one year taking place in some part of India. Indian holy days are more than a day off for the locals, they are a reason to spend time with friends and family… and, in India, socializing always involves food.

Holi (the festival of colours) is all about streetfood, which will vary from region to region; Diwali is vegetarian and also varies; in Kerala, every year they celebrate Onam with a vegetarian feast all eaten on a banana leaf; Eid is celebrated with the tastiest lamb, mutton or goat dishes; and Christmas will be celebrated with fish in some areas and pork in others (though both will have Christmas cake). The only thing this festive food has in common is that it will always be special and delicious.

There are plenty of high days as well, as someone is always graduating, getting engaged, married, or having a child. Traditionally, on these special days, the women congregate in the kitchen with the oldest member of the extended family delegating and also cooking with the rest.

In our home, a biryani was always considered special – it's great party food. Most Indians will cook a variety of different dishes, served altogether: normally a curry, some stir-fried and spiced vegetables and some rice, bread and raita. In Bengal they serve just one dish per course, starting with fried vegetables, moving to rice, lentils and then fish, chutney and dessert in an elegant meal. Special occasions in Kashmir can consist of 36 small courses that are very meat-heavy and eaten sitting on the ground. And the lovely Gujarati vegetarian thalis involve small portions of everything you need in a meal.

There is an old Indian saying that a guest is like a god and you should treat them in the same way, with respect and the best and warmest hospitality. When I was 12, my father decided to send us to boarding school in Simla. After visiting the school, we ate in a little café where my father chatted with the owner. The next day we had a bad car accident, hitched a ride on a bus and walked to the local hospital. When we were discharged, the café owner was waiting for us outside the hospital (he had seen us going in). He took us to his home and his wife made us chai and food while my father borrowed his phone. It was a gesture of pure kindness. My father did not send us to school there… as they say, the gods work in mysterious ways.

These days, India is changing. When people do entertain, things are often simpler; what I cook for friends gets less elaborate as life gets busier, and no one wants to leave the table too full. Don't feel obliged to stick with tradition. Do what works for you and remember to have fun!

Family trips to Goa are becoming a bit of a regular event over the Christmas holidays; I like my children to spend time regularly in India, and Goa is my spiritual home there. I have eaten lots of Christmas pastries, curries and so on while there, but one of the most special dishes to eat at Christmas is a small roasted piglet, marinated in Goan spices. I have used the same spices to cook a Christmas ham and added an East-meets-West glaze that works so well (East-meets-West is actually a defining characteristic of Goan food). I have decorated the ham with flaked almonds instead of the customary cloves and I find the crunch works really well and makes the ham feel special in its own way. **Serves 8**

Spice-glazed Goan-style ham

Start with the ham. Blend together the garlic, ginger, vinegar and powdered spices until smooth.

Place the gammon in a pot large enough to hold it comfortably. Add enough water to cover the joint. Bring to the boil, then skim off any scum that forms. Once the water is clear, add the spice blend, onion, bay leaf and black cardamom, if using. Cover and simmer gently for 20 minutes per 500g (1lb 2oz) depending on your joint. In this case cook for 3 hours 20 minutes, or until the internal temperature reaches 68°C (155°F). Lift the ham out of the water and leave to cool for 15 minutes.

Meanwhile, stir together the ingredients for the glaze. It should be thick enough to hold its form, but easily spreadable.

Preheat the oven to 220°C/425°F/gas mark 7.

Slice the skin but not the fat off the joint, using a sharp knife. Place in a roasting tray, adding about 2cm (¾in) of the cooking liquor. Brush just over half of the glaze over the top and place in the oven. Bake for 20–30 minutes or until beautiful and golden, basting every 8–10 minutes or so with the pan juices. Sprinkle over the almonds and, once they brown, take out. Tent with foil and leave to rest as you make a light sauce.

Heat up the rest of the glaze with a large splash or two of the roasting tray juices and bring to the boil. Allow to bubble, thicken a little and darken; it should be a bit thicker than a jus but not too thick. Taste and serve with the ham.

For the ham
8 large garlic cloves
30g (2 tbsp) finely grated root ginger (peeled weight)
2 tsp white wine vinegar
2 tsp freshly ground black pepper
2 tsp ground cumin
5kg (11lb) unsmoked, ready-soaked gammon joint (ideally bone-in)
1 onion, sliced
1 dried Indian bay leaf
2 black cardamom pods (optional)

For the glaze
150g (generous ½ cup) jaggery or light muscovado sugar
¾ tsp roast and ground cumin seeds (see page 184)
2 rounded tsp garam masala (fresh if possible, see page 113)
3 tsp finely grated root ginger (peeled)
3 small garlic cloves, crushed
6 tsp Dijon mustard
4 tsp Worcestershire sauce, plus more if needed
½ tsp freshly ground black pepper
large handful of flaked (slivered) almonds (optional)

The king of Indian (restaurant) curries, butter chicken is a velvety, tomato-based curry with little nuggets of lightly charred tandoori chicken hiding in its creamy depths. I have so many memories of eating this dish that I think we must have ordered it every time we went to an Indian restaurant! My two Delhi favourites were served at Moti Mahal and The Embassy and, later, the restaurant at The Park Royal where I spent some time learning in the kitchen. The recipe does have a few steps, and you can cheat by buying ready-made tandoori chicken or pastes, but it won't be as good or as satisfying. This sauce has a lot of tomatoes, so the end product will depend on how sweet or sour the tomatoes are. You will need to taste and adjust the final dish as necessary, adding more or less sugar depending on how tart or sweet the sauce is. Serve with Naan (see page 197) or paratha for a delicious and satisfying meal. **Serves 4**

Classic butter chicken

Blend together the ginger and garlic using a little water to help the blades turn.

Heat the oil and half the butter in a large non-stick saucepan over a medium-high heat and add the whole spices. Once they have sizzled for 15 seconds, add the ginger and garlic paste and cook until all the moisture has evaporated and the garlic smells cooked and looks grainy. Add the tomatoes and cook down until the resulting paste releases oil, around 20 minutes.

Now you need to brown this paste over a gentle heat, stirring often, until it darkens considerably, 6–8 minutes. Add 250ml (1 generous cup) water, bring to the boil, then pass through a sieve, trying to extract as much liquid and flavour from the tomatoes and spices as you can. Discard the very few, very dry solids. Set the sauce aside.

Cut or peel large chunks off the chicken pieces and reserve with any juices and charring that is still on the cooking foil.

Heat the remaining butter, throw in the green chillies and cook for 1 minute. Add the sauce, salt and a good splash of water and simmer for 3–4 minutes. Add the chicken, with any juices and charring from the foil. Add the sugar, chilli powder, paprika, fenugreek and garam masala. Simmer, stirring often, for 3–4 minutes, adding a little water if it is too thick. It should be lightly creamy. Take off the heat and stir in the cream, then taste and adjust the salt, sugar, cream or butter to taste as you need.

For the chicken pieces

6 skinned, bone-in chicken joints, cooked as for Tandoori-style Chicken (see page 60), but cooked for 18 minutes and not seasoned with chaat masala or fenugreek

For the butter chicken

20g (1½ tbsp) finely grated root ginger (peeled weight)
8 large garlic cloves
2 tbsp vegetable oil
80g (5½ tbsp) unsalted butter, plus more if needed
1 bay leaf
2 black cardamom pods
6 green cardamom pods
2cm (¾in) cinnamon stick
4 cloves
600g (1lb 5oz) vine tomatoes, blended to a fine purée
3–4 small green chillies (chiles), stalks removed, pierced with a knife
salt
1 tsp sugar, or to taste (depends on the sweetness of the tomatoes)
¼–½ tsp chilli (chili) powder
1 tsp paprika
2 tsp dried fenugreek leaves, finely crushed with your fingers
1 rounded tsp garam masala (fresh if possible, see page 113)
80–100ml (⅓–⅖ cup) single (light) cream, to taste

The Kutch are people from Gujarat. It is a small community and one I only heard about when my brother became really close friends with one of them in university. He often told me how delicious their food was and what a great cook his mum is. I think at some point he even wrote down a chicken curry recipe for me to try to cook... but I don't think I ever did. However, in Mumbai I tried some Kutchi food and it is indeed delicate, fresh and fragrant. Their chicken biryani is probably one of their more famous dishes and, while it has a few steps as does any biryani, it is fun and easy to do. You can put the whole thing together in advance and simply heat it through when you are ready. You can also just make the chicken curry separately; it is just as good. **Serves 6–8**

Kutch chicken biryani

Start with the marinade. Blend together the yogurt, ginger, garlic, chilli powder, garam masala, turmeric, salt, herbs and 1 tbsp oil until smooth. Pour into a non-reactive glass or ceramic bowl. Add the tomatoes and the chicken, mix well and leave to marinate as you cook the rice.

Rinse the rice under several changes of water or until the water remains clear when left in a bowl with the rice. Soak for 15 minutes.

Heat half the ghee in a large heavy-based saucepan. Add the cinnamon, bay leaves, 4 each of the green cardamom pods and cloves and half the peppercorns; cook until the spices puff up a little. Add the rice and sauté in the spiced ghee for 2 minutes. Add 1 litre (generous 4 cups) water and salt to taste (the water should taste well seasoned). Bring to the boil, then cover and cook very gently for 5 minutes. The grains should be only slightly undercooked in the middle. Take off the heat.

Now for the onion, to serve. Heat up 5cm (2in) oil in a very small saucepan. Add the sliced onion and fry until golden brown, then remove with a slotted spoon and place on kitchen paper to blot off the excess oil. Once dry, they should crisp up. Set aside. Remove and reserve the oil (you can use this in cooking for the next few days and it will impart a lovely onion flavour to the food).

Heat the remaining ghee and 2 tbsp of the onion oil in a large non-stick pan. Add the remaining green cardamom pods, cloves and peppercorns and the black cardamom pods and cook until these puff up. Add the finely chopped onion and fry until soft and browning at the edges. Then add the chicken with its marinade. Bring to the boil, cover and simmer until the masala has dried, 20–25 minutes. Stir occasionally. Once the moisture has dried up and it has released oil back into the pan, increase the heat and stir-fry the meat in the masala for a few minutes to intensify the flavours. The chicken should be done by now; if not, add a small splash of water and continue to cook, covered, until the chicken is cooked. When done, adjust the seasoning and take off the heat. There should be a little sauce in the pan – it shouldn't be too dry.

Continued on page 112

For the marinade

125g (scant ½ cup) Greek yogurt

30g (2 tbsp) finely grated root ginger (peeled weight)

10 large garlic cloves

⅓–⅔ tsp chilli (chili) powder, or to taste

1 tbsp garam masala (fresh if possible, see page 113)

¾ tsp ground turmeric

1 tsp salt

30g (1½ packed cups) coriander (cilantro) stalks and leaves

12g (generous ½ packed cup) mint leaves

3 tomatoes, skinned if you have time (see page 128), roughly chopped

For the biryani

1kg (2lb 4oz) skinned, bone-in chicken joints, cut into large pieces by the butcher

550g (3 cups) basmati rice

4–5 tbsp ghee

5cm (2in) cinnamon stick

2 dried bay leaves

8 green cardamom pods

8 cloves

1 tsp black peppercorns

2 black cardamom pods

1 large onion, finely chopped

Continued on page 112

Heat 1 tbsp more of the onion oil in a small saucepan, add the almonds and raisins, if using, and fry for 1 minute or until the raisins have puffed up and the almonds have browned Set aside. Rinse the pan out. Add the saffron, stir-fry gently for a minute, then add the milk, simmer for a minute or so and set aside.

Now you need to layer up the biryani in an appropriate-sized pan or oven dish. You can have as many layers as you like; traditionally it is 5 in total. Choose your pot or dish. Start by spooning in one-third of the rice, then spoon over half the chicken, add the next layer of rice, then the chicken then the last layer of rice. Drizzle over the saffron milk.

Cover with a tight-fitting lid, making sure nothing escapes the lid. Place on the flame, turn the heat up and cook for 2 minutes on a high flame and then 10–15 minutes on a very low flame. (You can also cook this in a preheated 180°C/350°F/gas mark 4 oven for 20–30 minutes.) When you can see steam under the lid, you will know everything is well heated through. Serve garnished with the fried sliced onions, toasted almonds and raisins, if using.

To serve
vegetable oil, as needed
1 medium-large onion, thinly sliced
handful of flaked (slivered) almonds
2 tbsp raisins (optional)
3 tbsp milk
good pinch of saffron threads

A Hyderabad biryani differs from most others across India. It is called "raw", as the meat is marinated overnight, then cooked with the rice from raw. It is delicate, fragrant, subtle but flavourful. The tastiest biryani I have ever tried was at the home of Nawab Mehboob Alam Khan, a Hyderabadi of regal bearing, with an interest in food that matched my own. The table was weighed down with the best Mughlai Hyderabad dishes: proper kormas, a whole kid goat surrounded by rice, haleem, stuffed roasted chicken, knuckle soup, kebabs, their own square naans and of course the biryani, which was so big it had to be carried by two men. A sword-like knife broke the seal on the lid... and dinner was served. This biryani is special for a reason: it takes time to prepare and has several stages, but is worth it! The green papaya helps to tenderize the meat, so I like to buy one for this and often grate and freeze the rest. **Serves 4**

A proper Hyderabad lamb biryani

Heat 5cm (2in) of oil in a saucepan and deep-fry the onions slowly until just brown and crisp. Remove with a slotted spoon and place on kitchen paper. Reserve the oil.

Wash the lamb well and prick it all over with the point of a knife. Place it in a bowl and add the papaya paste, salt, black pepper, chilli, garam masala, black cumin, lemon juice, ginger and garlic pastes, yogurt, 3 tbsp of the onion oil and two-thirds of the onions, crushed in your hands (if the onions are still soft in places, don't worry about it).

Now add the cardamom pods, cloves and cinnamon and half the coriander and mint taken from the amount for the biryani. Mix with your hands to help combine the flavours. At this stage you can leave

For the biryani
vegetable oil, as needed
2 onions, thinly sliced
500g (1lb 2oz) lamb (ideally bone-in), lean pieces of leg are ideal
handful of chopped coriander (cilantro) leaves and stalks
handful of chopped mint leaves
200g (1½ cups) chapati flour, or strong bread flour
500g (2¾ cups) good basmati rice
3 cloves

it to marinate, covered, overnight in the fridge, or for a few hours, depending on how much time you have.

When you are ready to cook, place the meat in a heavy-based pan and allow to return to room temperature. Make a firm dough with the flour and around 150ml (⅔ cup) water: you should be able to stretch it, but it should be firm. Roll into a sausage as long as the circumference of the mouth of the pan.

Wash the rice really well in several changes of water and soak for 18–20 minutes.

Meanwhile, place a large pot of water (the water should be 15cm/6in deep) to boil with the remaining whole spices, herbs and 2 tsp of the lemon juice. Season well, it should taste salty.

Heat the saffron in a dry pan until crisp and add the milk, bring to a simmer and cook for 1–2 minutes. Take off the heat.

Add the soaked rice to the spiced and seasoned water. Return it to the boil and then start timing. The rice needs to come off in 2½–3 minutes. Meanwhile, place a sieve over a bowl in the sink. When done, drain the rice through the sieve into the bowl. Spoon the rice over the meat in the pan.

Add 100ml (½ cup) of the hot rice water to the saffron with 4 tbsp more of the onion oil and pour evenly over the rice. Scatter over the remaining onions. Place the lid on top and seal with the dough. (It looks like a snake of dough sealing the lid with the pan.)

Place over a medium-high heat and, after about 7 minutes, you might be able to hear the steam build up in the pan. Reduce the heat to its lowest, using a heat diffuser if you have one, and cook for 50 minutes. Turn off the heat and allow to sit for 10 minutes.

Pull off the dough and serve, slightly mixed through.

5cm (2in) cinnamon stick
6 green cardamom pods
2 tsp lemon juice
large pinch of saffron threads
4 tbsp whole milk

For the marinade
½ tbsp green papaya paste (remove the skin and grate the flesh only)
1¼–1½ tsp salt
¼ tsp freshly ground black pepper
½ tsp chilli (chili) powder, or to taste
1 rounded tsp garam masala (fresh if possible, see below)
¾ tsp black cumin seeds (shahi jeera), lightly pounded
2½ tbsp lemon juice
10g (2 tsp) finely grated root ginger
4 large garlic cloves, finely grated
110g (½ cup) plain yogurt
6 green cardamom pods
3 cloves
5cm (2in) cinnamon stick

Garam masala

Place all the spices except the cumin and nutmeg in a large frying pan over a low heat. Stir often enough that the spices dry out but don't actually toast – 3–4 minutes. Add the cumin and nutmeg and toast for 30 seconds.

Pour straight into a spice grinder and grind until fine. Pass through a sieve over a bowl and discard any coarse pieces. Place these back in the grinder and grind again until fine. Store in an airtight container away from light.

10g (⅓oz) cinnamon sticks
10g (⅓oz) cloves
10g (⅓oz) green cardamom pods
7g (¼oz) black cardamom pods
2 dried bay leaves
7g (¼oz) black peppercorns
3 pieces of mace
10g (⅓oz) cumin seeds
½ nutmeg, grated (optional)

Green papaya

If you walk along the streets of Hyderabad, you will see stand after stand of limes, green papayas and fresh herbs. While this conveys the idea of a refreshing salad, really they are there because the people of this city love meat, and these ingredients feature regularly in their meat dishes.

In India, green papaya is used mostly as a meat tenderizer. This dark green, pear-shaped fruit with its almost translucent, light yellow flesh has little flavour of its own, but contains precious enzymes that efficiently break down the fibres of meat so that – once cooked – it melts in your mouth. This is particularly important for grilled meats, or meats which cannot simply stew to tenderness.

As with other fresh ingredients, green papaya is also known to be very good for us. It protects the body from free radicals and strengthens immunity, and is believed to be great for skin as well as the heart. Papaya and its seeds are thought to possess anti-amoebic and anti-parasitic characteristics, which are helpful for the bowel.

To use, peel off the skin, as this will be bitter. You don't need a lot of papaya to marinate meat, but the green papayas you find in the UK are generally very large, so I often make a healthy green papaya salad or a thoran with the main body of the fruit, keeping a few cubes in the freezer for future marinating use as, once you start marinating meat with green papaya, it is hard to go back!

This is a really elegant and delicious Bengali vegetarian dish called dhokar dalna. I tried it on my first trip to Calcutta, where I was taken to Kewpies for a proper Bengali meal. It was such a revelation and this dish stuck out as a lovely vegetarian main for friends. It consists of diamonds of blended chana dal – which looks like set polenta – fried and added to a lightly flavoured sauce which is more soup than curry and with very restrained spicing. It looks like a long recipe, and there are several steps, but none of them take very long and this can be on the table in less than 30 minutes. You would normally see some fried potatoes added to the dish, but I have left them out so the lentil cakes are the star. I normally serve this when friends are coming round, but you can eat it more simply with some rice and crispy fried vegetables on the side. **Serves 4**

Bengali lentil cakes in a mildly spiced sauce

Drain the lentils and blend to a coarse paste using only 2 tbsp water along with the salt, ginger, chilli and turmeric. Heat 2 tbsp oil in a karahi or non-stick saucepan, add the paste and cook, stirring and scraping the base constantly until it leaves the sides of the pan and forms into a ball, 3–5 minutes. It shouldn't be too dry or crumbly; if it is add a little water. Scrape into a wide bowl or even a plate, patting it into a 3.5cm (1½in) thick circle. Leave to cool and wash the pan.

Heat 7.5–10cm (3–4in) vegetable oil in the same pan. Slice the dal "cake" at 5–7.5cm (2–3in) intervals into diamond shapes. It shouldn't be crumbly; if it is, pat a little into place. Add to the hot oil (in batches if necessary) and fry over a medium heat until crispy and golden all over. You will need to give the pot the occasional stir, so the diamonds don't stick on the base, and so that they get an even colouring. Take out with a slotted spoon, allowing the excess oil to drip back in the pan. Place on kitchen paper to drain. Repeat to cook the remaining cakes, if needed. Drain out the oil, leaving only 3 tbsp in the pan.

Make the sauce. Heat this 3 tbsp of oil and add the asafoetida, bay leaf, cumin seeds, cloves and cinnamon stick. Cook until these have puffed up and the cumin has coloured. Add the blended onion and some salt. Cook, stirring often, until the onion has browned to a golden colour and tastes cooked rather than raw. Add the ginger and stir-fry for another 20–30 seconds. Add all the ground spices with a good splash of water and cook for 2–3 minutes. Take off the heat and add the yogurt, then return to the heat and constantly stir vigorously until the yogurt comes to the boil and reduces a little. Add 500ml (2 cups) water and the green chillies and return to the boil. Simmer for 5–6 minutes. Taste and adjust the seasoning, adding some black pepper and the sugar as well.

When you are ready to serve, place the dhokar in the sauce and simmer for 5–6 minutes to allow them to absorb some of the sauce. There should still be a fair amount in the pan, if not add some boiling water, adjusting the seasoning accordingly. Sprinkle with coriander.

For the lentil cakes (dhokar)
250g (1¼ cups) chana dal, soaked overnight, or for a few hours
1 tsp salt
12g (scant 1 tbsp) finely grated root ginger (peeled weight)
½–1 Indian green finger chilli (chile), stalk removed
½ tsp ground turmeric
vegetable oil

For the sauce
small pinch of asafoetida
1 large Indian bay leaf
⅔ tsp cumin seeds
2 cloves
2.5cm (1in) cinnamon stick
1 small onion, blended with a little water to help
12g (scant 1 tbsp) finely grated root ginger (peeled weight)
1 rounded tsp ground cumin
2 tsp ground coriander
½ tsp ground turmeric
⅛ tsp chilli (chili) powder
½ tsp garam masala (fresh if possible, see page 113)
2 rounded tbsp plain yogurt
4 green chillies (chiles), whole, stalks removed
freshly ground black pepper
¾–1 tsp sugar, or to taste
chopped coriander (cilantro), to serve

Biryani is one of India's most elegant and elaborate party dishes, and Hyderabad is well known for her meaty version. The original biryani was made with lamb, but this soon extended to chicken when it gained popularity (much later), or seafood in coastal regions. Vegetarian biryanis were created for impoverished royalty in some states, but also to cater for India's millions of vegetarians. This version is as delicate as any other biryani, where the rice is as important as the protein. Serve with a raita and, if you want, a vegetable side dish. I like to serve this with pan-fried aubergines with seasoned Greek yogurt and topped with pomegranate seeds, coriander and mint leaves. **Serves 6**

Hyderabad-style chickpea biryani

Put the saffron in a small cup with the milk and soak while you get on with the dish. Make the rice. Wash it really well in several changes of water, or until the water runs clear. Leave to soak.

Heat 1 tbsp vegetable oil and the ghee in a large, heavy-based, lidded pan. Add the whole spices and bay leaf and cook for 30 seconds or until aromatic. Add the onions and ½ tsp salt and cook until soft, stirring occasionally, then increase the heat and cook until golden. Drain the rice and add it to the golden onions. Stir well over a high heat to dry off any water and coat the rice in the oil for 2–3 minutes. Pour in the measured water, taste and season well. The water should taste a little salty, or the rice will be a bit flavourless. Bring to the boil, then cover and reduce the heat right down. Cook undisturbed for 6 minutes, then taste a grain; it should be nearly or just done. Take off the heat and set aside, covered, for 5 minutes. Spoon on to a large plate so it doesn't overcook. Set the pan aside for the final assembly.

For the chickpeas, blend together the tomatoes and yogurt. Heat 3 tbsp vegetable oil in a large pan. Add the onions with a good pinch of salt and cook until really soft, then increase the heat and cook until properly golden. Add the ginger and garlic and cook gently for 40–50 seconds. Add the ground spices and a splash of water and cook until the water has evaporated. Add the blended tomato mix and cook over a highish flame, stirring constantly, until the mixture comes to the boil and then reduces to a thick paste. Reduce the heat a little and cook until the paste darkens. Add the chickpeas and enough water to come halfway up the chickpeas. Return to the boil, taste and adjust the salt. Simmer for 5–6 minutes. Add the mint and coriander, and season for a final time. There should be some liquid in the pan; if not, add a little boiling water, or reduce if needed, until you have a watery curry.

To finish, place half the butter cubes in the pan. Cover with half the rice, then drizzle with half the saffron milk. Pour over the chickpea masala and top with the remaining rice, saffron and butter. Cover tightly with a lid and cook over a really low heat for 20–25 minutes or until steaming. Scatter with crispy onions and coriander.

For the rice
400g (2¼ cups) basmati rice
vegetable oil, as needed
2 tbsp ghee
5 cloves
5 green cardamom pods
2.5cm (1in) cinnamon stick
1 dried bay leaf
2 small onions, thinly sliced
salt
750ml (3⅛ cups) water

For the chickpeas
2 medium tomatoes, roughly chopped
4 tbsp plain yogurt
2 small onions, finely chopped
1 good tsp finely grated root ginger
4 large garlic cloves, finely grated
¼–½ tsp chilli (chili) powder
2 tsp ground coriander
2 tsp ground cumin
½ tsp ground turmeric
2 tsp garam masala (fresh if possible, see page 113)
2 x 400g (14oz) cans chickpeas (garbanzo beans), drained and rinsed
3 tbsp chopped mint leaves
3 tbsp chopped coriander (cilantro)

To finish
large pinch of saffron threads
4 tbsp hot milk
20g (1½ tbsp) unsalted butter, cubed
large handful of storebought crispy fried onions and chopped coriander (cilantro), to serve

The Mughals came to India in the 1500s. The word is derived from the Persian word for Mongols, who were descendants of Genghis Khan. Genghis and his sons conquered Central Asia, came as far into Europe as Poland, through Persia and eventually to India... although by the time they came to India, they had more civilized Persian sensibilities than those of their famous ancestor. The Mughals ruled parts of India for hundreds of years; the last Mughal emperor was finally deposed by the British and sent to Burma in exile in the 1800s. It is therefore no surprise that the Mughal love of meat, kebabs, breads and refined food lives on and has become as synonymous with Indian food as lentils. This curry is inspired by Mughal cooking. White poppy seeds have a delicious flavour and add a little creaminess, but if you can't find them, add ground almonds to the sauce (and loosen with water), or a little single cream. **Serves 4**

Mughlai-style braised lamb shanks

Blend together the ginger and garlic with a little water until smooth. Set aside. In the same jug, blend the yogurt and tomatoes together.

Heat the oil in a large pan. Add the shanks and brown on all sides; this is not traditional, but I like to do it as I prepare all the other ingredients. Remove and place on a plate.

Add the whole spices and cook until they puff up a little. Add the onions with a pinch of salt and cook until they are soft and a good golden brown on the edges. Add the ginger and garlic paste and cook gently for 1–2 minutes or until the garlic smells cooked and is colouring. The onions should be a lovely colour now. Add the tomato-yogurt paste, the cumin, chilli powder, coriander and half the garam masala.

Cook, stirring every now and again, and more so as it thickens, until it releases oil back into the pan. Then stir-fry for a few more minutes. Add in the lamb and cook in the sauce for a few minutes. Add enough water to come one-third of the way up, bring to the boil, then cover and cook gently until the lamb is cooked and very tender. I like to stir the pot pretty often, maybe every 15 minutes or so, this helps to homogenize the sauce, and I top up the water whenever it looks low but I never add too much at any one time. It should take around 2 hours on a medium-low to medium heat, but can take longer if the heat is too low.

Meanwhile, grind the poppy seeds to a fine paste. Set aside.

When the lamb is tender, take off the cover. Remove the shanks and place on a plate. Cook off some of the excess liquid, then add the poppy seed paste and cook for a few minutes. Taste and adjust the seasoning, add the julienned ginger and the remaining garam masala, then return the shanks. Coat well in the creamy sauce, cook for a few minutes and serve sprinkled with coriander and almonds, if using.

25g (1½ rounded tbsp) roughly chopped root ginger (peeled weight)
8 large garlic cloves
100g (⅖ cup) plain yogurt
3 large tomatoes, washed and quartered
4 tbsp vegetable oil
4 lamb shanks, (each about 400–450g/14oz–1lb)
5 cloves
5cm (2in) cinnamon stick
5 green cardamom pods
1 mace blade
½ tsp black peppercorns
¾ tsp caraway seeds
3 small onions, thinly sliced
salt
2 tsp ground cumin
¼–½ tsp chilli (chili) powder, or to taste
2 tsp ground coriander
2 rounded tsp garam masala (fresh if possible, see page 113)
1½ tbsp white poppy seeds, soaked in a little water
20 strands or so of julienned root ginger
good handful of chopped coriander (cilantro), to serve
roasted flaked (slivered) almonds, to serve (optional)

I worked in the restaurant of the Park Royal Hotel in Delhi in the very early days of exploring my passion for Indian food. On one of the very first days, the chef was making chicken with fenugreek. We ate a fair amount of fenugreek at home, but never with chicken, so I was curious to see what it tasted like. Obviously, it was excellent and although I didn't take the recipe or follow what the chef was doing properly, the flavour memory stayed with me. A decade later, I decided to cook it for my father, the real gourmet of the family. This is how I made it. It is really nice to have a dish that is recognizable in its origin, yet a little bit different to other Indian dishes you have tried. If you can find fresh fenugreek, that would add more flavour, but I always have a packet of dried fenugreek leaves and they make this truly delicious. I add a knob of butter at the end, to give the dish that enriched restaurant feel. Serve with Indian breads. **Serves 4–5**

Chicken with fenugreek

Blend together the tomatoes and yogurt until smooth.

Heat the oil in a large non-stick saucepan or karahi. Throw in the whole spices and fry for 30 seconds. Add the onions and a good pinch of salt and fry until soft and browning. Add the ginger and garlic and cook, stirring often, for another minute or so. Spoon in the ground coriander, turmeric and the chilli powder and give the pan a few good stirs.

Add the blended tomatoes and season well with salt. Stir constantly as it comes to the boil to stop it from splitting. Once it is bubbling, stir every now and again to make sure it doesn't stick to the base of the pan. You will need to stir more as it thickens.

Once the masala releases oil back into the pan, add the chicken pieces. Stir and cook for around 8 minutes, then add enough water to come halfway up the chicken. Bring to the boil, cover and cook gently for 15 minutes or until the chicken is done.

Crumble in the dried fenugreek leaves and stir in the garam masala. Cook for another few minutes over a high-ish flame, reducing the sauce until it is quite thick and clingy. Taste and adjust the seasoning, stir in a knob of butter (if using) and serve.

4 small tomatoes, quartered
200g (¾ cup) plain yogurt
6 tbsp vegetable oil
2 black cardamom pods
5cm (2in) cinnamon stick
1 dried Indian bay leaf
5 green cardamom pods
5 cloves
2 medium-small onions, finely chopped
salt
30g (2 tbsp) coarsely grated root ginger (peeled weight)
8 large garlic cloves, coarsely grated
2 tsp ground coriander
¾ tsp ground turmeric
½ tsp chilli (chili) powder, or to taste
1kg (2lb 4oz) skinned, bone-in chicken joints, cut into large pieces by the butcher
7 tbsp dried fenugreek leaves, or to taste
2 good tsp garam masala (fresh if possible, see page 113), or to taste
knob of unsalted butter (optional)

Fenugreek leaves

The fenugreek plant yields both leaves and seeds that are used in Indian food. The seeds are small, beige and hard and are used sparingly in curries and spice blends as have a strong flavour and a bitterness to them. The leaves are pretty little things and – all bunched together – they look like a verdant and innocuous bouquet… but this appearance is really deceptive as, once you cook them, they are flavoursome and have their own edge of bitterness.

Fenugreek leaves are another cure-all elixir in traditional Indian medicine. They are considered to have strong anti-viral and anti-oxidant properties, so they are thought to be great for general good health. However, they are also believed to be helpful in the treatment of almost everything, including arthritis, reducing cholesterol levels, maintaining a healthy heart, treating asthma and bronchitis, healing skin problems (wounds, rashes and boils) and sore throats. An Ayurvedic doctor would add that fenugreek leaves are detoxifying for the body, while new mums are given fenugreek leaf-laced meals to help with the production of breast milk.

Fresh fenugreek leaves are sold in bunches in Indian supermarkets. Wash them well before use and cook with only the leaves, not the stalks. Don't feel that you have to use the whole bunch immediately, as they freeze very well; I often grab a handful of frozen leaves and add them straight to the pan (you can also now find frozen packets in some Indian markets). This herb is wonderful with fish, chicken, lamb, paneer, potatoes, worked into dough and added to rice.

You can also buy dried fenugreek leaves (*kasturi methi*). These aren't a poor substitute – in fact they are often less bitter and more aromatic than fresh, and are used extensively as a distinctive herb. They are an important ingredient of tandoori food, many breads, or in curries for an added layer of flavour. I always have a box at home and often add large pinches to my cooking. You can replace fresh leaves with dried, as they are easier to find and can reside in your larder. I have cooked my Chicken with Fenugreek (see page 120) using the dried leaves; if you would rather use fresh leaves, you need to up the quantity by roughly 2.5 times.

A word of caution: fenugreek leaves are thought to bring on labour, so pregnant women are traditionally steered away from eating them, as well as from fenugreek seeds.

A kadhai – a certain spice combination – is both a type of restaurant dish and also a cooking pot, similar to a wok but with rounded sides. It is a really useful pot as it allows you to stir-fry with without worrying about bothersome edges, but also to cook a curry and do everything else you need in an Indian kitchen. The word kadhai also refers to the dish's style and the spices used. This is a delicious and versatile sauce to have with any protein, but also works really well with vegetables, and is one of the dishes I order for my vegetarian husband in Indian restaurants (in India). Delicious with Indian breads, Naan or Flaky Malabar Paratha (see pages 197 and 195). **Serves 4**

Mixed vegetable kadhai

In a small frying pan, gently dry-roast the spices for the kadhai masala, stirring often to avoid any burning. Once the coriander seeds have coloured a little, pour everything into a spice blender and grind to a fine – or even slightly coarse – powder.

Heat the oil in a large non-stick saucepan, add the onion and cook until golden on the edges. Add the ginger and garlic and sauté for 1 minute or until they smell cooked. Add the blended tomatoes, turmeric and salt and cook over a medium-high heat until the mixture has completely reduced and releases oil back into the pan.

Stir in the potato and carrot, cover and cook gently for 5 minutes. Add the cauliflower and boiling water and return to the boil. Cover and cook for another 15 minutes or until the vegetables are just cooked, adding the peas for the last couple of minutes.

Add the garam masala and fenugreek leaves to the pan and give it a stir. Take it off the heat and sprinkle over and shake in the cream and coriander. Taste and adjust seasoning and serve.

For the kadhai masala
1 tbsp coriander seeds
¾ tsp cumin seeds
1–2 Kashmiri dried chillies (chiles) (these are mild, if you don't have them, use 1 red chilli, or give them a miss)
8 black peppercorns

For the sauce
4 tbsp vegetable oil
1 large onion, finely chopped
5g (1 tsp) finely grated root ginger (peeled weight)
3 large garlic cloves, finely grated
3 medium-large tomatoes, blended until smooth
½ tsp ground turmeric
salt
½ tsp garam masala (fresh if possible, see page 113)
1 tsp dried fenugreek leaves, crushed between your fingers
2–3 tbsp single (light) cream
3 tbsp chopped coriander (cilantro) leaves, to serve

For the vegetables (this is the classic version, but vary them as you like)
1 potato, cut into 2cm (¾in) pieces
1 small carrot, cut into half moons
100g (3½oz) 3–4cm (1½in) cauliflower florets
480ml (2 cups) boiling water
100g (⅔ cup) frozen peas, defrosted

AUTO PRIDE

CAR WASH

Auto Pride Carwash - SanCarlos
195 El Camino Real
650-591-4638

09/18/21, 05:44 PM   Cashier1,
Shift 1, Emp1 3278,   Sale # 13882312704

---

1 Cook Books   29.99

Subtotal   29.99
Sales Tax   2.81
Total   32.80

Discover x6154   32.80
(Sale Appr # 01808P)

"Sindhi" refers to a group of people who had to leave their home town of Sindh in Pakistan upon the partition of India. Growing up, many of my Indian friends were Sindhi, so I had many occasions to eat their food. Like all Indians, they love good food but they also love to entertain – and do so very well. Their tables are always laden with more than a handful of dishes, all a little different from other regional food. Yet this koak palla dish is one I have missed and only just learned about recently.

The Sindhi people use palla fish, an oily, meaty river fish with thick flesh. I like butterflied whole fish and have tried it with gurnard and sea bream, but also with halibut steaks. I have written the recipe for one fish so you can scale it up for however many you want to cook. Here I have used fillets of fish which are a good option for guests who might feel a little squeamish with whole fish and fish bones. **Serves 1–2**

Sindhi-style grilled fish

If you have a fan-assisted grill (broiler) function on your oven, turn it on fairly high, around 220°C/425°F/gas mark 7. Otherwise, preheat the oven and turn on the grill at the same time or – if you can't do that in your oven – preheat your oven to as high as it will go.

Pulse-blend together the onion, garlic, ginger, spices, yogurt and three-quarters of the tomatoes to a very coarse paste. Stir in the coriander, chilli and remaining tomatoes. Season well with salt and pepper.

Heat the oil in a large non-stick frying pan over a high heat. Season the flesh side of the fish. Once hot, add the fish, flesh side down: it will spit. Cook for 1–2 minutes or until lightly golden. Take off the heat and flip on to a baking sheet or some foil, flesh side up.

Meanwhile, in the same pan, add the blended ingredients and stir-fry over a high heat for 3–5 minutes or until the paste releases oil back into the pan. It should taste harmonious. Adjust the seasoning and heat to your own liking. Top the fish evenly with the paste. Place on the upper shelf of the oven, under the grill if possible, and cook for 6–7 minutes or until the topping is dried and has lightly browned in places. After about 6 minutes, l like to sprinkle with the optional breadcrumbs (see below). Serve hot.

Optional crispy topping

I like to tear up some white bread (one-quarter of a slice for 1 fish) into 5mm (¼in) pieces, add a little olive oil (if you want to be more fancy, you can make a coriander oil by whizzing coriander in it) and toss. Add this to the top of the fish 30–40 seconds before taking the fish out.

½ onion, chopped
2 large garlic cloves, finely grated
7g (½ tbsp) finely grated root ginger (peeled weight)
1 tsp ground coriander
1 tsp ground cumin
⅓ tsp garam masala (fresh if possible, see page 113)
¼ tsp ground turmeric
1 rounded tbsp Greek yogurt
1 tomato, chopped
small handful of coriander (cilantro), to serve
small Indian green finger chilli (chile), finely chopped
salt and freshly ground black pepper
2 tbsp vegetable oil
1 medium gurnard, sea bream or other whole fish, butterflied by the fishmonger, or a fish steak, or even a thick fish fillet

There are probably more lentil dishes in India than there are combined in all other cuisines around the world. Although lentils were considered the poor man's protein, they are so intertwined with an Indian meal that you will find enriched dal dishes on menus in every Indian restaurant, and cooked in Indian homes around the world. This is a really delicious, typically restaurant-style version, therefore thicker and richer in flavour than a home-style dal. It goes with so many different dishes, from vegetables to kebabs, that you just can't go wrong. This is best served with Indian flatbreads though, as it is too thick to serve with rice. If your tomatoes are not very sour, add some dried mango powder (amchur) or lemon juice; I generally add a little to sharpen up the flavours anyway. **Serves 4**

The best tarka dal

Rinse the lentils in several changes of water to wash well. Place in a large pot and pour over enough water to come 5cm (2in) over them. Bring to the boil, then skim off all the scum that forms on the surface. Add the turmeric and ginger and continue to boil for 20 minutes, or until the lentils are just soft. You might need to add some water if it cooks off.

Meanwhile, score the base of each tomato with a knife, put them in a bowl and pour boiling water over them. Leave for 30 seconds, then drain off the water. Their skins should just slip off. Chop and set aside.

Heat the oil in a non-stick saucepan. Add the asafoetida, cinnamon, cloves and dried chillies and cook for 10–15 seconds or until they puff up. Spoon in the cumin seeds and cook until they colour and smell roasted. Add the onion and cook until it has golden edges. Add the garlic and cook, stirring for 1 minute, or until it smells cooked.

Now tip in the tomatoes, salt and ground spices (except the dried mango powder) and cook over a high heat for 10 minutes, stirring and mashing them often, or until the masala releases oil into the pan. If the tomato is dry, you will need to add a splash of water from the kettle to help.

By now the lentils should be cooked and, when stirred with a spoon, the water and lentils should start to become homogenous and slightly creamy. Pour some into the tarka pot with the onion and chillies, then pour it all back into the lentils, making sure you scrape every last bit of flavour from the saucepan.

Cook for another 3–5 minutes to bring it all together, adding the butter to enrich the dal. Stir in the chopped coriander, then taste and adjust seasoning, adding the dried mango powder to taste if you would like it a little more tart.

150g (¾ cup) yellow lentils (mung dal)
50g (¼ cup) chana dal
½ tsp ground turmeric
20g (1½ tbsp) finely grated root ginger (peeled weight)
3 medium-small tomatoes
2½ tbsp vegetable oil, or ghee, or both
tiny pinch of asafoetida
2.5cm (1in) cinnamom stick or cassia bark
4 cloves
1–2 dried chillies (chiles)
1 rounded tsp cumin seeds
1 small onion, finely chopped
5 large garlic cloves, finely chopped
salt
¾ tsp ground cumin
1½ tsp ground coriander
¾ tsp garam masala (fresh if possible, see page 113)
knob of unsalted butter
good handful of chopped coriander (cilantro)
½–¾ tsp dried mango powder (amchur), or to taste (optional, see introduction above)

This is one of the dishes my mother would make on special occasions, but it is also a really popular cooling and nutritious streetfood. The tastiest version I have eaten is in Old Delhi in the large market of Chandi Chowk, which is known for its streetfood. I make a big batch of the dahi bhalla dumplings and freeze them, so I can put together this dish fairly easily in less than 10 minutes. This is quite a taste sensation in the mouth: sweet, savoury, soft and spongey and creamy all in one bite. Also, it is much lighter than it seems, as the batter doesn't absorb much oil.

This is quite a traditional recipe but you can add other bits on top, like pomegranate seeds. Here, I cook up 25 so I can freeze half for another occasion, but make up only half the quantity if you prefer; people normally eat one or two each maximum. **Makes 25 (can be halved)**

Delhi-style lentil dumplings in yogurt

Drain off most of the water from the lentils, leaving 2–3 tbsp, and place in a blender. Add the ginger and green chilli and grind until the batter is pretty smooth (though it m ... ... some tiny granules in it). You can add water if necessary to ... ... water you add the better. The batt...

Heat about 7.5cm (3in) oil i... It needs to be medium hot. ...

Add the baking powder, co... extra whisks to incorporate...

Place a bowl of water near... up a large walnut-sized an... ease it off, let it slide into ... oil for it not to splash up. ... you may need to fry the ... or until lightly golden. R... excess fat and place on ...

When you are ready to ... recently boiled hot water for ... the water. Meanwhile, whisk together the yogurt, meas... salt, sugar and roast cumin until smooth. The mixture should be the consistency of single (light) cream.

Add some cold water to the dumpling bowl so you don't burn your fingers, and gently squeeze out the water. A lot of oil comes out as well. Place straight into a serving bowl or plate.

Spoon over the yogurt so the dumplings are covered, then spoon or drizzle over first the tamarind chutney and then the coriander chutney, so each dumpling has some of both. Serve or refrigerate to use later. It is served both at room temperature and chilled.

For the dumplings
210g (1 cup) urad dal (split and skinned black lentils), soaked overnight
... (2 tsp) finely grated root ginger ...eeled weight)
... 1 Indian green chilli (chile), ...talk removed, or to taste
...getable oil
... tsp baking powder
...mall handful of chopped coriander (cilantro)
...⁄4 tsp salt

To make up half of them (for 12 dahi bhalla)
450g (1¾ cups) plain yogurt
90–110ml (⅓–½ cup) water
salt
3 tsp sugar, plus more if needed
¾ tsp roast and ground cumin seeds (see page 184)
Proper Date and Tamarind Chutney (see page 181), to serve
Tangy Herb Chutney (see page 182), to serve

I love okra – it is such a great vegetable, not too watery, not too starchy, not too metallic and really good for you. I have never found it "gluey" when cooked properly, despite its unfair reputation. There are so many ways to cook it, but I do love it in this aachari bhindi, and it is really easy to cook. These spices and simple sweet, tart flavours add masses of flavour to a simple vegetable. It is a slightly tangy recipe and works well with any meat, chicken, fish or lentil dish. **Serves 4–6**

Four seed-spiced okra with tomatoes

Heat the oil in a large non-stick sauté pan over a medium heat. Add the seeds and, once they are popping, add the onions and green chillies and cook until the onions are browned on the edges and soft.

Add the okra, tomatoes, seasoning and remaining ground spices and stir to mix well. Cover and cook for 10–12 minutes or until the okra is soft and cooked through, giving the pan a stir every few minutes.

Taste and adjust the seasoning, adding more dried mango powder if you would like it a bit more tart, then add the coriander and serve.

4 tbsp vegetable oil
¾ tsp nigella seeds
¾ tsp cumin seeds
¾ tsp brown mustard seeds
¾ tsp fennel seeds
3 small onions, finely chopped
1–3 Indian green finger chillies (chiles), stalks removed, pierced with a knife
400g (14oz) okra, stalks sliced off
4 tomatoes, chopped
salt
¾ tsp ground turmeric
1 tbsp ground coriander
½–¾ tsp dried mango powder (amchur), or to taste
handful of chopped coriander (cilantro), to serve

Regional stars

I once met a man of Indian heritage in Australia. Born in Singapore, he didn't know which part of India his family was from. I delved into what his family had eaten when he was growing up and the conclusion was that they must have been from the south or south west of India. As an Indian, I feel I can often guess which region someone comes from by what they eat at home. In reality, the truth is more complex...

The early roots of Indian foods were deeply influenced by the Ayurveda advocates of ancient times, who recommended mostly vegetarian diets, meals that were healthy and easy to digest, with vegetables, pulses and added healing and digestive spices. After that, the food was defined by what grew locally and seasonally, but was later influenced by the colonizers, traders and settlers from different countries.

The Moghuls of Central Asia were among the first to arrive. They were used to cooler climates, few spices, a meat-heavy diet, breads, and lots of grilling and roasting. They brought these preferences with them and, over the years, their dishes were Indianized. The result is fusion food which we now call Mughlai food. This might not be strictly regional, but it is one of India's best-loved cuisines.

The food of Kerala is known for its abundance of coconuts, seafood and spices. In addition, Kerala was a key trading port and attracted a variety of settlers over the years. Arab traders came for the spices but ended up staying and marrying local women. The result is a fusion of Arab, Muslim and Southern Indian cooking, known as Moplah food. The Syrian Christians arrived as missionaries and converted many locals; now almost one-third of the population of Kerala is Christian. Their own dishes tend to be milder, and include roasts, which – in oven-free India – are usually pot-roasted. The food of Kerala is often known as Malayali food.

The Portuguese colonizers of Goa insisted that the Goans convert to Catholicism and embrace their culture, including their love of pork. They also brought chillies, pineapples, cashew nuts, tomatoes and pumpkins as well as a baking tradition that still exists today...

Another group of influential immigrants were the Chinese, and the streets of Kolkota are filled with momos: steamed Nepalese-Chinese dumplings served with a chutney or broth. A lot of Indo-Chinese fare has made it into the mainstream, such as sweet-and-sour sauces that coat everything from chicken to paneer.

The Parsis were exiled from their home in Persia and came to Gujarat. Their food is a combination of Persian and Gujarati, but, while Gujarati food is known for its vegetarian thali, Parsis are almost exclusively meat-eaters; even their vegetable dishes contain meat, or at the very least, eggs.

Such is the multi-layered nature of India and its cuisine: a collection of regional cuisines that has been influenced by people from across the globe, as they spice up the dishes they love.

Karnataka has lots of delicious food, but this is one of those dishes that people outside the region hear about. Maybe this is because India has so few pork curries... or maybe it's because it is that good. This dish comes from the cooler hills of Karnataka. The people of that area were forced to hunt for food and got a taste for wild boar. Soon, many locals started to farm their own pigs, to be sure they could have this local favourite whenever they wanted! In spite of all the spices, this isn't an overtly spicy curry. I have added Kashmiri chilli powder more for colour than heat, so you can leave it out if you prefer. **Serves 4**

Slow-cooked Karnataka pork curry

Blend the ginger, garlic and tomato until fine, adding a little water to help the blades turn. Set aside.

Heat the oil in a large non-stick pan. Add the mustard seeds and, once the popping calms down, add the curry leaves, onions and 1 green chilli; cook until really well browned. Add the blended paste, the turmeric, salt, cumin and chilli powder, if using, and cook well until all the liquid has reduced and the remaining masala releases oil, around 10–12 minutes.

Meanwhile, dry-roast the spices for the spice blend for 40–50 seconds, or until lightly golden. Pour straight into a mortar and pestle and grind to a fine powder.

Add the pork to the masala in the pan and brown a little in the paste. Add 3 tsp of the spice blend and the vinegar. Bring to the boil, then cover and simmer really slowly, stirring often and checking to see if you need to top up the water (if so, use boiling water from the kettle). Cook until the pork is really tender, anything from 1 to 2 hours; I've done it in both, and it really depends on the heat.

Taste, adjust the seasoning, adding more of the spice blend if you like, stir in the coriander and serve hot with rice or Indian breads.

For the curry
15g (1 tbsp) roughly chopped root ginger (peeled weight)
7 large garlic cloves
1 tomato, quartered
3 tbsp vegetable oil
½ tsp brown mustard seeds
15 curry leaves
2 medium-small onions, finely chopped
1–3 green chillies (chiles), stalks removed, pierced with a knife
½ tsp ground turmeric
salt and freshly ground black pepper
1 tsp ground cumin
½ tsp Kashmiri chilli (chili) powder (optional)
500g (1lb 2oz) pork shoulder, cut into cubes, with some fat
3½–4 tsp white wine vinegar
handful of coriander (cilantro) leaves and stalks, to serve

For the spice blend
1½ tsp cumin seeds
2 tsp coriander seeds
3 small cloves
5mm (¼in) cinnamon stick
1 tsp fennel seeds
10 black peppercorns
pinch of brown mustard seeds

Parsis came to India from Persia hundreds of years ago, fleeing persecution, but a legend says that the Indian ruler didn't want to let them in, saying, "We are full." The Parsi asked the ruler to bring a bowl and fill it up to the brim with milk. He then added a spoon of sugar. The cup did not overflow. "We will be like the sugar," he said. "We will only add sweetness to your country." And indeed they did, and are now a very respected part of the community. Parsi food is not only influenced by its Persian roots but also by the British and the Indians. This is one of their better-known dishes.

I visited a well-known Parsi restaurant in Mumbai a few years ago. The owner has a giant portrait of The Queen. When he found out we were from England, he spent a good amount of time chatting with us. He recommended this chicken dish topped with salli: crispy fried potato straws. **Serves 4**

Parsi salli chicken

Heat the oil in a large non-stick saucepan over a medium heat. Add the onions and cook until soft. Then increase the heat and cook, stirring often, until golden brown. Add the ginger and garlic and cook gently for 1 minute, or until the garlic smells cooked.

Pour in the blended tomatoes, then add the seasoning and all the ground spices. Cook down until the masala releases oil, about 15–20 minutes. Taste – it should be harmonious.

Tip the chicken into the masala along with a good splash of water. Bring to the boil, then cover, reduce the heat and cook for 25–30 minutes or until the chicken is cooked through. Give the pot occasional stirs as it cooks and check that there is enough water in the pan. At this stage you can make the Crispy Potato Salli (see page 140).

Taste and adjust the seasoning and consistency of the sauce, which should have a light, creamy consistency. If it is too watery, cook over a high heat until thickened to your liking, or add some water from a boiling kettle to loosen a little. Stir in the coriander, sprinkle with Crispy Potato Salli and serve.

4 tbsp vegetable oil
2 onions, finely chopped
5g (1 tsp) finely grated root ginger (peeled weight)
5 large garlic cloves, finely grated
3 large vine tomatoes (400g/14oz), blended until smooth
salt and freshly ground black pepper
¾ tsp ground cinnamon, or to taste
2 tsp garam masala (fresh if possible, see page 113)
½ tsp ground turmeric
¼ tsp chilli (chili) powder, or to taste
1 rounded tsp ground cumin
6–8 medium-small skinless bone-in chicken thighs (1.25–1.3kg/2lb 12oz–3lb in total)
handful of coriander (cilantro)
large handful of Crispy Potato Salli (see page 140), or as much as you like

You can add some sliced almonds to the rice, but  I love it like this with its sweet, buttery saffron flavours contrasted with the sweet–sour cherries. **Serves 4**

Parsis love these delicate, crunchy potato ... they are really moreish ... flavours of the Parsi ... an make ... r 4

Parsi rice with saffron and sour cherries

300g (1¾ cups) basmati rice
⅓–½ tsp saffron threads
2 rounded tbsp ghee or unsalted butter
2 large cinnamon sticks or cassia bark
6 green cardamom pods
10 black peppercorns
handful of dried ready-to-eat sour cherries
600ml (2½ cups) water
salt
handful of halved pistachios (optional)

Wash the rice really well in several changes of water until the water runs clear and all the starch has been removed, then soak for about 15 minutes. Infuse the saffron in 1 tbsp boiling water for the same time.

Heat the ghee or butter in a large, heavy-based pot. Add the whole spices and cook for 20 seconds or until they are aromatic. Meanwhile, drain the rice in a sieve. Tip the rice into the pan and give it a few stirs. Add the saffron and cherries and give the pot a couple of stirs. Add the measured water and salt, taste and adjust the seasoning.

Bring to the boil, then reduce the heat right down, cover tightly and cook for 7–9 minutes. Check a grain, it should be cooked through, if not cook for another couple of minutes. Scatter over the pistachios, cover again, turn off the heat and allow the rice to steam for 10 minutes. Serve with Parsi Salli Chicken (see page 138).

Peel the potatoes, slice thinly widthways, then line up some of the circles and slice into short matchsticks. (To slice my potato, I use the slicer on my box grater.) However you do it, try to slice them evenly. Place on a dish towel and pat dry.

Heat 7.5cm (3in) of oil in a wide, deep saucepan or in a deep-fat fryer to a medium heat (dip a shred of potato in: it should sizzle). Add the potatoes in batches, being careful not to overcrowd the pan. Cook over a medium heat until the potatoes are crispy and golden. You will need to carefully separate any clumps that stick together with a fork quite early on. Each batch will take 2–3 minutes. Remove using a slotted spoon and place on a plate lined with kitchen paper. Repeat to cook the rest.

Sprinkle over salt and chilli powder to taste and toss well to combine.

This has a fair amount of heat, but the flavour is so good and the chicken so soft that you can't stop eating! My mother's friend used to make something similar with chicken on the bone and I just couldn't stop eating even as it made me sniff and tear up; it was that good. No one knows why it is called chicken 65, as the origins of the recipe are really blurry, but it is a well-known and much loved dish in Andhra. There are a couple of versions – one with a sweet chilli sauce added to it and others with a vibrant red food colour. I leave both out, but sometimes add some Kashmiri chilli powder to the marinade, which has a lovely colour but only mild heat. **Serves 3**

Andhra green chilli chicken 65

Mix all the ingredients for the marinade together in a large bowl. Taste, adjust the salt and add the chicken. Marinate for at least 30 minutes, but longer in the fridge would be better (return to room temperature before cooking).

Beat the egg and cornflour into the chicken and marinade.

In a deep, wide pan over a high heat, heat about 5cm (2in) vegetable oil. Once it is hot enough to fry with, add one-third of the chicken; it should sizzle as soon as it hits the hot oil. Cook over a high heat for 3 minutes, turning once, or until the chicken is deeply golden on both sides. Remove with a slotted spoon and place on kitchen paper to blot off the excess oil. Repeat to cook all the chicken.

Pour the oil through a sieve into a small bowl. Return 2½ tbsp back to the pan and heat through. Add the curry leaves and cook for 20 seconds or until they are crisp. Add the ginger, garlic, green chillies and a good pinch of salt and stir-fry for 1 minute, then add the chicken and black pepper and stir-fry over a high heat for another 30 seconds to bring the whole thing together.

Taste, adjust the seasoning and serve immediately with lemon wedges.

For the marinade
4 large garlic cloves, finely grated
10g (2 tsp) finely grated root ginger
  (peeled weight)
1 tsp ground cumin
⅓ tsp Kashmiri chilli (chili) powder
  (optional, see introduction above)
¼ tsp ground turmeric
1½ tsp ground coriander
4 tsp lemon juice
40g (3 tbsp) plain yogurt
⅔ tsp salt

For the chicken
2 chicken breasts, cut into
  2cm (¾in) pieces
1 egg
2 tbsp cornflour (cornstarch)
vegetable oil, as needed
25 fresh curry leaves
20g (1½ tbsp) finely chopped root
  ginger (peeled weight)
3 large garlic cloves, finely chopped
3–6 Indian green finger chillies
  (chiles), to taste, 1 finely chopped,
  2–5 just pierced with a knife
good grinding of freshly ground
  black pepper
lemon wedges, to serve

When the name of a dish means something to a non-native speaker, you know it is special. Although chickpea curries abound in many regions across India, this famous version hails from Amritsar. The city is best known for its very beautiful Sikh Golden Temple, but also for the truly delicious food. Even the vegetables there have so much flavour because – it is claimed – the local water itself is sweet and tasty. Chickpea curry is the city's iconic dish, finished with a knob of local white butter, red onions and julienned ginger and served with their famous stuffed bread (see page 150). It is a fabulous combination... but I can tell you from experience that this curry is equally delightful with lightly buttered brown toast. **Serves 4–5**

Amritsari chana masala

Heat the oil in a large saucepan, add the onion and a little salt and cook until it has browned on the edges. Meanwhile, blend the tomatoes with a little water until smooth.

Add the ginger and garlic to the cooked onion and sauté for 1 minute or until they are just colouring. Add the ground turmeric, cumin and coriander, the chilli powder and garam masala and cook for 20–30 seconds before adding the tomatoes. Cook over a medium heat, stirring occasionally, until the oil is released into the pan, around 15 minutes, stirring often.

Meanwhile, toast the cumin seeds in a small pan, stirring very often, until they have darkened and smell aromatic, around 40 seconds. Grind to a fine powder and add to the pot.

Add the chickpeas and a little more salt and give the pot a good stir. Add enough boiling water to come to the top of the chickpeas. Bring to a simmer and cook for a few minutes.

Taste and add the dried pomegranate powder or tamarind paste: you will need less if your tomatoes were sour; more if they were sweet. Finish off with the chopped coriander, taste and adjust the seasoning.

Serve with a small knob of butter, ginger julienne and a scattering of red onion for the real Punjabi experience.

5 tbsp vegetable oil
1 onion, finely chopped
salt
2 medium-large tomatoes, quartered
18g (1 rounded tbsp) finely grated root ginger (peeled weight)
4 large garlic cloves, finely chopped or grated
½ tsp ground turmeric
1 tsp ground cumin
1 tbsp ground coriander
¼–½ tsp chilli (chili) powder, or to taste
1½ tsp garam masala (fresh if possible, see page 113)
1 tsp cumin seeds
2 x 400g (14oz) cans of chickpeas (garbanzo beans), drained and rinsed
⅓ tsp dried pomegranate powder (anardana), or tamarind paste, or to taste
handful of finely chopped coriander (cilantro)

To serve
knob of unsalted butter
a few ginger julienne
small sprinkling of finely chopped red onion, to serve

Tamil food is little known in this country beyond the well-known Crispy Masala Dosa and Tamil-style Lentil and Vegetable Curry, or sambhar (see pages 156 and 153), but the food from this region is so good. It has amazing seafood dishes, as this southernmost region is surrounded on three sides by the Arabian Sea. But further inland it is also known for its black pepper- and chilli-laced, fiery – but so moreish – recipes. Add the black pepper to taste; you can always add extra at the end if you want it. This isn't a watery curry – the gravy clings to the meat, so serve with flatbreads and a cooling raita. **Serves 4**

Southern peppery Chettinad chicken

Start with the marinade. Blend together all the ingredients for the marinade until smooth and place in a large non-reactive bowl. Add the chicken, coat well in the marinade, cover and leave to marinate for as long as possible; covered overnight in the fridge is best. Return to room temperature before starting.

Heat the oil in a karahi, wok or large saucepan. Add the curry leaves and follow 10 seconds later with the onions and a little salt; sauté until well-browned on the edges.

Add the tomatoes, ground coriander and cumin and garam masala and cook for 4–5 minutes over a high-ish heat, stirring a bit. Add a splash of water if the tomatoes are dry. Add the chicken with the marinade and black pepper and cook, stirring often, for 20 minutes, or until the paste releases oil back into the pan. Add enough boiling water to come halfway up the chicken, bring to the boil, then cover and simmer for another 10–15 minutes, or until cooked through. Taste and adjust the seasoning and serve.

For the marinade

20g (1½ tbsp) roughly chopped root ginger (peeled weight)

4–5 large garlic cloves

1–2 dried chillies (chiles), deseeded and soaked for 30 minutes

1 tbsp lemon juice

½ tsp ground turmeric

1 tsp salt

For the chicken

700g (1lb 9oz) skinless, bone-in small chicken joints, cut into large pieces

5 tbsp vegetable oil

15 fresh curry leaves

3 small onions, finely chopped

2 tomatoes, chopped

1 tbsp ground coriander

1 rounded tsp ground cumin

1 rounded tsp garam masala (fresh if possible, see page 113)

2–3 tsp freshly coarse-ground black pepper, or to taste

Paneer

This simple, homemade white cheese is normally set into a block, then cut into cubes before being cooked. The flavour is similar to a fresh white farmer's cheese, a bit like ricotta. It is a quintessential north Indian ingredient, as dairy is abundant in that region and the people love good food, whether meat-based or not.

Paneer was sometimes thought to be the poor man's protein as meats were, and still are, comparatively expensive – too much for most people to eat every day. However, Punjabis and many others absolutely love paneer, regardless of their wealth and eating habits.

It is an extremely versatile ingredient and lends itself to so many different styles of dishes. The textures can be played with (they can be dense, soft, crumbly or even spongy); however, in any form, this lovely fresh cheese works with all Indian flavours really well.

You will find it eaten at breakfast as a vegetarian spiced scrambled "egg" served with buttered buns; you can eat it spiced and grilled from a tandoor oven or a barbecue, such as with my Grilled Herby Paneer Parcel

(see page 68); it can be layered inside breads, cooked into curries or stir-fried. You can eat it in Indo-Chinese Chilli Paneer (see page 170), or it can even be fashioned into desserts: think cheesecake, but without the complex carbs.

Paneer is easy to find in Western supermarkets now, but it is simple and really satisfying to make yourself. All you need is milk, yogurt or lemon juice, and a muslin/cheesecloth or a clean J-cloth (for the recipe, see page 184). Once made, paneer can be stored in the fridge in a container of water. When you are ready to cook with it, soak it in seasoned boiling water for 20 minutes to help soften the texture; especially important if you plan to grill the cheese.

The Bengalis are known for their love of fish and, in fact, add it to anything they can; this rice dish is a great example. The fish heads not needed in their beloved curries are saved and cooked in this delicious muri ghonto recipe, or with lentils. This rice has a gentle flavour of fish and the heads have long been considered a really healthy delicacy. If you just can't see yourself eating – or even wanting to see – fish heads, you can replace them with a couple of fish steaks which you sear well in a pan and finish cooking in the rice. **Serves 4**

Bengali fish head rice

Clean the fish heads inside and out. Sprinkle over the turmeric and season lightly, rubbing all the seasonings into the fish. Place the potato into a bowl of well-salted water and set aside.

Heat the mustard oil in a small non-stick saucepan until smoking. Remove from the heat and allow to cool for 10 seconds (or heat the vegetable oil as normal). Add the fish heads and fry on both sides until golden, around 3 minutes a side. Take out the fish with a slotted spoon and set aside. Slice in half when cool enough to handle (so each half has an eye).

Drain the potatoes, then pat dry. Add them to the oil and cook until golden all over, around 3 minutes (they won't be cooked through). Remove with a slotted spoon and set aside with the fish.

Add the onion and green chillies and cook until the onion is just colouring on the edges, then tip in the ginger and garlic and sauté gently until these are just starting to colour. Now add the ground spices, seasoning and a splash of water from the kettle and cook until the water has evaporated. Throw in the tomato and cook down until the paste releases oil back into the pan, 5–6 minutes.

Add the drained rice and stir well in the paste for 3–4 minutes. Pour in the measured water, potatoes and fish heads. Season the water to taste. Return to the boil, then reduce the heat, cover and cook for 6–8 minutes or until the rice is cooked through. Serve hot.

3 fish heads (I use sea bream)
¾ tsp ground turmeric
salt and freshly ground black
  pepper
1 small potato, peeled and cut into
  2cm (¾in) cubes
3–4 tbsp mustard oil, or vegetable
  oil
1 red onion, finely chopped
2–3 green chillies (chiles), stalks
  removed, pierced with a knife
12g (scant 1 tbsp) finely chopped
  root ginger (peeled weight)
3 large garlic cloves, finely chopped
1 rounded tsp ground cumin
1½ tsp ground coriander
1½ tsp garam masala (fresh if
  possible, see page 113)
1 medium-large tomato, chopped
175g (1 cup) basmati rice, rinsed
  well and soaked
300ml (1¼ cups) water

Amritsar has a particular flaky, tandoor-cooked bread stuffed with potatoes or paneer, onions and spices. It is one of the dishes I sought out in Amritsar and, when you eat the real version, you understand why they are eaten there for breakfast, lunch and dinner. They are crisp outside and soft within with lots of distinct flavours and textures. Eating them fresh on a bustling street with a cup of masala tea was one of my most memorable Indian breakfast experiences. This is as close to the original as I could get without a tandoor oven and it is really moreish. It is normally made with plain flour, but I sometimes make it with chapati flour so it is healthier; or I mix the two. This bread is also amazing cooked on a barbecue: just brush with a little ghee or butter before serving. **Makes 10**

Spiced potato-stuffed Amritsari kulcha bread

Start with the dough. In a bowl, mix together all the dry ingredients. Add the 2 tbsp ghee and the smaller amount of water and bring it together, adding the remaining water if needed. The dough will sticky in the beginning, but it will absorb t is kneaded. Divide the dough evenly into towel and leave to rest for around 1 hour.

Meanwhile, mix together the ingredients hands, almost squashing the potatoes in mostly smooth and homogenous. Taste a

Dust a work surface with flour and take your fingers, dust more flour on top and round. Brush or smear with ½ tsp ghee. take about one-tenth of the filling (arou over the top. Pat down into a thin layer edges clean.

Taking one edge, roll, Swiss-roll style, a little to elongate into a longer rope. N charmer would, into a spiral, and pres little flour to roll each bread out into a medium don't want the filling to peep through but, if it does, it is OK. Cover with a damp dish towel. Repeat to form and stuff the rest.

Heat a tava or frying pan over a high heat.

Place a bread coil on the pan and cook for 20–30 seconds, then flip over; if it is sticking, use a spatula to loosen any stubborn bits (it will be the filling poking out). Cook for another 20–30 seconds, smear the upper surface with a little ghee and flip over again. Now drizzle a little more ghee on this side and cook both sides until it has lovely golden swirls and is nice and crispy.

Keep warm while you repeat to cook the rest and ideally serve the straight away.

For the dough
300g (2⅓ cups) plain (all-purpose) flour, or chapati flour, plus more to dust

wder
s more to form

nt–generous

cooked floury
ally baked, or boiled
, or microwaved until
cubes
finely chopped

er seeds
seeds
½ tsp cumin seeds
½ tsp garam masala (fresh if possible, see page 113), or to taste
large handful of finely chopped coriander (cilantro)
½–1 Indian green finger chilli (chile), finely chopped
salt

Tea

Tea is a drink that most Indians could not live without, but it is a fairly recent addition to the Indian menu. Tea was introduced to India by the British during the domination of the East India Company. At that time, they were importing tea from China and bringing it back to England, but after many trade wars with China, the Company turned their focus to growing tea in India.

Soon they realized that Indians themselves didn't drink tea and – spotting a huge market – planned a strategy to introduce them to this humble leaf. Salesmen went from house to house with a lovely teapot and cups, teaching Indians how to brew and drink tea. The East India Company weren't one of the richest companies in the world for no reason; they knew how to mount a campaign and, soon, Indians were converted to drinking tea. However, much to the despair of the British, they were not brewing tea as they were taught, they didn't all go out and spend money on a teapot, and instead they threw the tea in a pan with some milk, ginger and spices and brewed what we know today as chai, or spiced tea.

Indians today are one of the world's biggest tea drinkers and Indian black tea is of a fantastic quality. You can hardly walk the streets of most Indian cities without bumping into a chaiwalla. When I was young, any time my mother took us shopping in India, the first thing you were offered was a cup of chai, bought from the local chaiwalla; it was very civilized. Sadly, fewer people drink tea in this part of the world now than ever before, with the drink becoming more and more unfashionable.

When I got married, I would throw a tea bag into a pot of brewing spices and milk for my masala tea fix. My husband's family – in the tea business for generations – were horrified and disapproving. Soon I was getting large vacuum-packed parcels of the finest black Assam sent to me by my father-in-law… and my entire tea-drinking experience changed. Comparing the depth of flavour from good-quality tea leaves to what we get in the typical tea bag in the UK is like comparing an instant coffee to a very well-brewed Italian cup. So now, my father-in-law's kindness has ruined my pleasure of having a decent cup of tea outside my home (aside from in some very well-stocked places). On the flip side, I am apparently ruining this amazing pure-flavoured tea he sends me, as I still insist on brewing it with a pot of milk (soy milk, no less) and a variety of spices like a proper Indian!

I was once told by a supermarket buyer that "a curry is a curry". This couldn't be further from the truth. A curry is a dish cooked with a sauce and it is Indian, so it will contain spices. However, to an Indian, "chicken curry" means different things depending on what region you are from. On top of that, my mother cooked a cumin-flavoured chicken, a yogurt-flavoured chicken, a dried pomegranate-flavoured chicken, and so on... The point is: Indians define a "curry" by both its region and the defining flavour.

Here, although the main spice note is green cardamom, it does not overpower the dish and the black pepper stops it becoming too sweet. For the green cardamom, I grind a fair amount with husks on (they are very aromatic, so worth adding) and use as I need. If your spice blender doesn't get the powder fine, add it to the dish through a sieve to catch the larger bits. Serve with Indian breads. **Serves 4**

Sindhi cardamom lamb

Blend together the tomatoes and yogurt until smooth.

Heat the oil in a large non-stick saucepan or karahi over a medium heat. Add the onion with a little salt and sauté until soft and starting to colour on the edges. Add the lamb and seal well over a high-ish heat for 4–5 minutes. Add the ginger, garlic and green chillies and cook over a low heat for another minute or so or until the garlic smells cooked.

Add the yogurt blend, the spices and a little more salt and bring to a simmer, stirring all the while. Once the yogurt is bubbling, you can stir only occasionally. As it thickens, you will need to stir more often to make sure it doesn't stick. You need to cook the yogurt down until it releases oil back into the pan; this can take 10–15 minutes.

Add enough water to nearly cover the lamb, bring to the boil, then cover and cook gently until the lamb is tender, another 40–60 minutes or so.

When the lamb is done, reduce the sauce if it is still watery (you want it to be creamy) by increasing the heat and stirring the meat in the sauce as it reduces. If it is too thick, add a little boiling water. Season to taste, adding more cardamom or black pepper if you like.

Stir in the coriander and serve.

2 tomatoes, quartered
120g (½ cup) plain yogurt
4–5 tbsp vegetable oil
1 red onion, finely chopped
salt
650g (1lb 7oz) lamb or mutton pieces, with a few pieces of bones if possible
20g (1½ tbsp) finely grated root ginger (peeled weight)
4 large garlic cloves, finely grated
2 whole green chillies (chiles), stalks removed, pierced with a knife
2 tsp ground coriander
1½ tsp ground green cardamom, or to taste (see introduction above)
⅔–¾ tsp freshly ground black pepper, or to taste
good handful of chopped coriander (cilantro), to serve

Sambhar is an everyday curry, eaten in slight variations across the Southern coast at almost any meal. It is served with steamed, fluffy saucer-shaped rice and lentil cakes – idlis – or crispy masala dosa, and a coconut chutney. When in India, my family regularly visited a temple about four hours' drive from Chennai, at the top of a range of hills. It is customary to walk from the base of the hills to the temple, which takes three hours, and the whole way you see people chatting, laughing, chanting, and full of hope and expectations. The temple has an amazing energy and you always leave elated. After the walk, we went for a meal in the local restaurant, Mayur, where dosa, idli, sambhar and coconut chutney were the order of the day. I love this so much that I often make it and eat simply with brown rice and coconut chutney. **Serves 4**

Tamil-style lentil and vegetable curry

Bring the lentils to the boil with half the turmeric and 1 tsp salt in enough water to cover the lentils by around 7.5cm (3in). Skim off any scum that forms on the surface, then simmer until the lentils are soft and break up in the liquid; around 45 minutes.

About 30 minutes in, heat the oil in a large non-stick saucepan. Add the asafoetida and, after 10 seconds, the mustard seeds. Once the popping dies down, add the curry leaves and chillies (if using). Stir well and, after another 10–15 seconds or so add the onion. Sauté until it has softened and turned brown on the edges, 8–10 minutes over a medium heat, stirring often. Add the garlic and sauté for 30–40 seconds. Add the remaining turmeric and three-quarters of the sambhar powder, then cook for 30–40 seconds.

The lentils should have broken down now; if not, give them a good whisk. Add the prepared vegetables and tomato to the soft lentils with the onion mixture from the saucepan and stir well, cover and cook for 6–7 minutes, stirring once or twice. Add the tamarind and cook for another 3–5 minutes, or until the vegetables are done.

Adjust the water content (it should be a thin curry), then taste and adjust the seasoning, adding sambhar powder and tamarind paste to taste. It should be tangy and have the wonderful flavour of the sambhar powder. Bring to the boil and cook for another 2–3 minutes, then serve.

125g (⅔ cup) split pigeon peas (toor dal), washed and soaked for 1–2 hours if possible
⅔ tsp ground turmeric
salt
2–3 tbsp vegetable oil
pinch of asafoetida
¾ tsp brown mustard seeds
10 fresh curry leaves, or 16–18 dried curry leaves
1–2 dried chillies (chiles, optional)
1 small onion, finely sliced
2 garlic cloves, finely chopped
2–3½ tbsp sambhar powder, or to taste (different brands have different strengths)
3 handfuls of prepared vegetables (in India they use 3–5 seasonal varieties, such as cauliflower, okra, green beans, drumstick, carrots, potatoes, summer gourds, aubergines/eggplants), all cut into large 5–7.5cm (2–3in) pieces
1 large tomato, quartered
1 tbsp tamarind paste, or to taste (different brands have different strengths)

The food from Andhra is some of the spiciest in India. The region has so many delicious lamb dishes, so it was hard to choose just one for this book, but in the end I chose this dish as I was struck by the flavourful and not-too-spicy fat green chillies grown in Andhra and used in abundance. You can find short, fat green chillies in the West and they are so good; some are spicier than others, so this is not for the faint hearted. The chillies add a really wonderful flavour but not too much heat; if you are unsure, push them to the side of your plate. I like to make sure there is at least one chilli per person, but you might want to add extra for those who love the heat. Serve with Indian breads. **Serves 4**

Tangy Andhra lamb with fat green chillies

Heat the 4 tbsp oil in a large non-stick saucepan. Tip in the cumin seeds and fry for 30 seconds, or until they darken a little, then add the onions and cook until soft and really well browned.

Meanwhile, blend together the tomatoes, ginger and garlic until nice and smooth.

Add the lamb to the pot and cook over a high-ish flame for about 1–2 minutes. Add the blended paste, salt, black pepper, ground turmeric and coriander and chilli powder (if using). Cook over a medium-high heat, stirring every few minutes, until all the liquid in the pan has cooked away and the pot looks quite dry, 10–12 minutes.

Add enough water to come halfway up the lamb, bring to the boil, then cover and simmer gently until the meat is tender, 50–70 minutes. Check on it every 10–15 minutes, giving it a stir and adding a splash of water if the pot seems dry.

As this cooks, individually dry-fry the sesame seeds and desiccated coconut until lightly golden. Pour both straight into a mortar and pestle, add the peanuts and grind to a fine powder. Set aside.

When the lamb is done, give the pan a wipe and add the remaining 1 tsp oil. Add the slashed chillies and stir-fry for 4–5 minutes or until the sides have changed colour. Add to the lamb with the powdered seeds and nuts, the garam masala and half the tamarind. Return to the boil and simmer for 4–5 minutes or until the chillies are just soft. Taste and adjust the seasoning and tamarind to taste, add some boiling water if the curry seems dry, and serve sprinkled with the coriander.

4 tbsp vegetable oil, plus 1 tsp for the chillies
1 rounded tsp cumin seeds
2 onions, finely chopped
2 tomatoes, quartered
15g (1 tbsp) roughly chopped root ginger (peeled weight)
4 large garlic cloves
600g (1lb 5oz) diced lamb
salt and freshly ground black pepper
½ tsp ground turmeric
2 tsp ground coriander
¼ tsp chilli (chili) powder (optional)
1 rounded tbsp sesame seeds
3 tbsp desiccated coconut
2 tbsp roasted peanuts
4–6 fat green chillies (chiles), a little slit cut in one side
2 tsp garam masala (fresh if possible, see page 113)
1 tsp tamarind paste, or to taste
handful of chopped coriander (cilantro), to serve

A dosa is a crispy rice and lentil pancake and is normally breakfast food for the locals in Tamil Nadu. These days we eat it for dinner. It takes a day or more to allow the batter to ferment, to give a slightly sour flavour and make it a little fluffy. There are so many different types of dosa, but this is the most popular, stuffed with a spiced potato masala and served with sambhar (a thin lentil curry) and Coconut Chutney (see pages and 153 and 180). But that is a lot to cook, so we normally have dosa with either potatoes or lentils. The dosa is gluten free, dairy free and fermented – all buzzwords for health these days. Oh, and it is really tasty and fun to make. My ten-year-old tried her hand at it while I was writing this recipe and we had a lot of fun. A dosa is best eaten as soon as it is cooked, so if you have guests over, eat with them at the kitchen counter while you make them. **Makes 9–10**

Crispy masala

Wash the rice well in several changes [of water until the water runs] clear, then soak it overnight or for 5– [hours. At the same time] wash the lentils well and leave them, [together with] lentils, reserving the water. Now grin[d] [the rice, lentils and] fenugreek seeds to a fluffy paste with [a blender, using some of] the reserved water. It should be smo[oth with no grain] grains left; this does take a few minu[tes. Cover and] leave to ferment in a warm-ish, drau[ght-free spot for a day] or so; it needs to start fermenting an[d rising.]

When you are getting ready to eat, m[ake the masala.] halve the potatoes and boil until jus[t soft, or prick, skin still] on, in the microwave and cook until soft. Once done and cool enough to handle, peel and roughly chop.

Heat the oil in a large non-stick frying pan. Add the mustard seeds and, once the popping starts to die down, add all the chillies and chana dal; following 10 seconds later with the urad dal and the curry leaves. Cook until the lentils are just golden. Add the onions and a little more salt, sauté these until golden brown on the edges, then add the ginger and cook for another minute or so. Add the turmeric and a splash of water and give the pan a couple of stirs. Add in the potatoes and mix well in the other flavours. Cook for 4–5 minutes, then add the lemon juice and adjust the seasoning. The potatoes should be slightly crushed and in large lumps rather than pieces now. Add the ghee if using and stir in the coriander.

Now cook the dosas. Choose a frying pan, ideally cast iron, but you can use a non-stick one as well. Find a 60ml (¼ cup) ladle or serving spoon. Heat the pan over a medium heat.

Take the half onion, spear it with a fork and dip in oil, then wipe the pan with the onion. Using your chosen ladle or spoon, add the batter to the middle of the pan, and quickly – using the base of the ladle – spread the batter out in circular motions before it sets. It should look

[For the dos]a
[...g (... c]ups) basmati rice
[...g (...)] urad dal (split
[and skinn]ed black lentils)
[...roundeds (...] tbsp) chana dal
[a pinch] of fenugreek seeds

[vegetable o]il, as needed
[Coconut C]hutney, to serve
[(see page] 180)

For the potato filling
750g (1lb 10oz, or around 4 medium) cooking potatoes
salt
5–6 tbsp vegetable oil
1½ tsp brown mustard seeds
2–4 dried chillies (chiles, optional)
2 Indian green finger chillies (chiles), halved
1 rounded tbsp chana dal
1 rounded tbsp urad dal (split and skinned black lentils)
15–20 fresh curry leaves
2 medium-large onions, thinly sliced
1½ tbsp finely chopped root ginger
1 tsp ground turmeric
1 tsp lemon juice, or to taste
1 rounded tsp ghee (optional)
handful of coriander (cilantro) leaves

quite thin in places, if not everywhere. The thinner, the crispier! Leave to cook over a medium heat, drizzling over 1 tsp of vegetable oil. It shouldn't take more than 2–3 minutes.

Once you can see brown coming through the thinner bits of the dosa and it is rising a little, check the base – it should be golden. Take it off the heat, fill with a few spoons of the potato filling and serve with Coconut Chutney. Repeat to cook the rest of the batter, eating each dosa as soon as it is cooked.

Mention sarson ka saag to any self-respecting Punjabi and they will become nostalgic about the last time they ate it. I didn't grow up in the villages of Punjab, but even I get transported to open fields of mustard greens, yellow cornmeal breads and fresh, homemade white butter... It is rich, so we don't eat it often – mostly for Sunday lunch so that there is time to digest it over the afternoon! I couldn't write a book of my favourite Indian recipes without it. You may not find all the greens you need for an authentic flavour, but you can find fresh mustard greens and a can of all the greens mixed together. This is normally served with cornmeal bread, but you can try it with Missi Roti or Flaky Malabar Paratha (see pages 196 and 195) – or even hot cornmeal tortillas with butter on them! **Serves 6**

Punjabi mustard greens

Boil the fresh greens for 10–20 minutes, until wilted. (In the Punjab they would be cooked for the longer time.)

Meanwhile, heat the ghee, or butter and oil, in a large non-stick saucepan. Add the onions and a little salt and sauté until browning, around 10 minutes. Reduce the heat to low, add the ginger and garlic pastes and continue to sauté until these are cooked and colouring; another 1–2 minutes. Add the tomatoes and sauté for 5–6 minutes, then follow with the spices and a little more seasoning and cook until the masala releases oil into the pan, around 10 further minutes over a medium heat, stirring often.

While the tomatoes are cooking, blend the cooked greens until smooth and add to the cooked tomatoes along with the contents of the can. Bring to a simmer, cover and cook for 15 minutes. Add the cornmeal and jaggery and cook for another couple of minutes, then serve with a little knob of butter, sprinkled with the julienned ginger.

450g (1lb) mustard leaves,
  stalks removed
150g (5½oz) large leaf spinach,
  stalks removed
3 tbsp ghee, or 2 tbsp unsalted
  butter and 1 tbsp vegetable oil
2 small red onions, finely chopped
salt
25g (1½ rounded tbsp) finely grated
  root ginger (peeled weight)
6 large garlic cloves, finely grated
2 tomatoes, chopped
2 tsp ground coriander
½ tsp ground turmeric
1 rounded tsp ground cumin
450g (1lb) can of sarson ka saag
  (see introduction above)
1½ tsp cornmeal
1 tsp jaggery or brown sugar,
  or to taste
knob of butter, to serve
julienned root ginger, to serve

Comfort food

One day in the first year of my marriage, we went to my parents' home for lunch, and mum cooked a typical Sunday lunch of chickpea curry and flatbreads. As I relished my mother's cooking after a bit of an absence, I noticed my husband ate little. I later asked him why… he said he didn't love the curry. Obviously that did not go down too well! A couple of months later, his mother cooked her version of the same dish; my husband, loving her food after a long absence, genuinely thought it was so much better. I didn't agree. It was just that we preferred what we were brought up on.

I love tasting new dishes. You can take me (almost) anywhere and I will be excited to eat there. However, there are those times when I'm tired, under the weather – or just because of the weather – when I seek comfort food. Like everyone else, this is the food I grew up on and, in my case, it is my mother's cooking. My children's comfort food could be anything, as they eat a variety of cuisines regularly, but I have been trying to socially engineer it so that their comfort food is Indian (brainwashing them, mostly). I want them to crave these healing and healthy flavours and ingredients long after time has rescued them from my meddling ways. Like all experiments, I don't know whether it will fail or succeed, but it is definitely worth a try!

Almost all Indian food is comfort food to someone. All across the country, mums cook dishes for their children that they themselves learned from their mothers. These are normally regional, seasonal, inexpensive, easy to make and rustic. Most of the recipes in this book could fit comfortably into this chapter, but those that have made it in are some of the most popular, warming and sustaining.

A quick word on the karahi: this is a pan similar to a wok but with rounded sides, so there are no edges. It is one of India's traditional pans and, as you stir the pot, food moves gracefully around without bits getting stuck in the edges. This is great, of course, for stir-fried dishes, but also for curries, as regular stirring of a masala as it cooks will ensure a homogenous and creamy sauce in which the ingredients melt into each other. In fact, traditionally, a new chef in a professional kitchen will spend most of his time stirring pots of curries, up and down the line, to ensure all the sauces have the best flavour and texture. Karahis also seem to work whether you are cooking for two people or four, as everything just pools in the centre. They are great pans, easily available in Indian shops and markets, and I recommend them for all avid cooks, Indian or not.

Chicken was not widely cooked in Hyderabad. In fact, it was considered unclean for a while, so red meats were the dominant protein. As a result, there are few traditional chicken dishes in Hyderabad but they do make chicken korma and they often pot-roasted it. I bake it in the oven, as it is easier. You can also add blanched almonds, blended with water, as that would normally be used to enrich the korma, but I add a little cream instead. Do blend the herbs to a fine paste if possible for a silky smooth sauce. Serve with Indian breads, sliced fried potatoes, vegetables or pilaf rice.
Serves 4–6

Hyderabad baked herby chicken korma

Blend together the ginger, garlic and yogurt and 1 tsp salt. Rub this under the skin of the chicken and leave to marinate for 1 hour, if possible. Pound the coconut in a mortar and pestle until it is powdery.

Heat 4cm (1½in) of oil in a small-ish saucepan over a medium heat. Add the onions and fry until golden and crisp on the edges. Drain off the oil and set aside.

Set aside a quarter of the onions and place the rest in the same blender container as you used for the yogurt mixture (no need to wash) along with 2 tbsp of the cooking oil (use the rest for cooking another dish, it will taste of delicious fried onions), the herbs, coconut, garam masala and lemon juice. Blend until smooth; you might need to add a little water to help the blades turn. Pour this over the chicken and mix well. Now, leave it for as long as you can to marinate, covered in the fridge, or at room temperature if it is just for 1 hour. If you are in a hurry, you can also just cook it now.

Preheat the oven to 180°C/350°F/gas mark 4. Place the chicken and marinade in a large baking dish that can take the chicken in a single, snug layer. Tuck in the chillies, if using.

Bake on the middle shelf of the oven until done, 40–45 minutes, basting every now and again. Once done, if the chicken doesn't have any colour, place on the upper shelf for 5 minutes or so.

Stir the cream into the pan juices and mix well. Taste and adjust the seasoning and lemon juice to taste. Serve hot, sprinkled with the reserved onions and extra coriander, along with potatoes, rice or Indian breads.

20g (1½ tbsp) roughly chopped root ginger (peeled weight)
6 large garlic cloves
275g (1 cup) Greek yogurt
salt and freshly ground black pepper
8 medium-small, bone-in, skinless chicken pieces (around 1.2kg/2lb 12oz)
4 tbsp desiccated coconut
vegetable oil
2 medium-large red onions, finely sliced
40g (1⅓ packed cups) coriander (cilantro) leaves and stalks, plus more to serve
20g (¾ packed cup) mint leaves (around 40g with stalks)
1 rounded tsp garam masala (fresh if possible, see page 113)
2 tsp lemon juice, or to taste
2–4 green chillies (chiles), stalks removed, pierced with a knife
4 tbsp single (light) cream

This dish is the pride of many Bengali homes. The recipe changes from cook to cook but fresh fish is always a requisite. The man of the house would normally go to the market, first thing in the morning before work, to buy the freshest possible fish. The light sauce – jhol – is more akin to a flavoured stock than a thick sauce. Use any firm, white-fleshed fish; you can use fillets, but you will not get the flavour that you would with a steak. Also, mustard oil really adds to this dish and is traditionally used, but you can use vegetable oil. Serve with Simple, Perfect Rice (see page 189). You can find Indian bay leaves in Indian stores or online; don't use regular bay leaves instead as they have a different flavour. **Serves 4**

Bengali sea bream with cauliflower

Wash the fish and rub in some salt and half the turmeric. Set aside for about 5–10 minutes. At the same time, salt the cauliflower florets and set aside.

Heat the oil in a large non-stick frying pan until it is smoking. Take it off the heat for 10 seconds to cool down, then add the fish. It will splutter, so have a lid close by. Fry until golden on both sides, about 5–6 minutes. Remove the fish with a slotted spoon, reserving the oil.

Blend together the onion, ginger, garlic, cumin and mustard seeds until smooth, adding a little water if necessary to help the blades turn. The seeds don't have to be completely fine, but do try and get it pretty smooth.

Heat up 3 tbsp of the mustard oil from the frying pan in a medium-large non-stick saucepan over a medium heat. Add the panch phoran and cook for 20 sizzling seconds or until the seeds have darkened. Now add the bay leaves and follow a beat later with the onion paste, remaining ground spices, chillies and some salt and cook until it releases oil back into the pan, 10–12 minutes, stirring occasionally.

Meanwhile, heat up the remaining oil in the frying pan over a low heat and add the cauliflower. Cook gently, turning often, until just softening, 5–7 minutes. Set aside.

Add the water to the masala. Bring to the boil and simmer gently for 5–6 minutes. Add the fish and return to a simmer. After a minute add the cauliflower, cover and again return to a simmer. Cook for another 3 minutes or until everything is cooked through.

Sprinkle over the coriander, taste and adjust the seasoning and serve hot with rice.

2 medium sea bream, cleaned, scaled and cut into 2.5–4cm (1–1½in) steaks (see introduction above)
salt
1 tsp ground turmeric
150g (2 cups) large cauliflower florets
4–5 tbsp mustard oil (preferably), or vegetable oil
½ red onion, quartered
20g (1½ tbsp) roughly chopped root ginger (peeled weight)
2 large garlic cloves
1 tsp cumin seeds
1 tsp brown mustard seeds.
½ tsp panch phoran
2 dried Indian bay leaves
2 tsp ground coriander
¼ tsp chilli (chili) powder, or to taste
½ tsp garam masala (fresh if possible, see page 113)
2–3 green chillies (chiles), stalks removed, pierced with a knife
400ml (1¾ cups) water
handful of chopped coriander (cilantro)

Goans love their pork and use every bit of it. Ribs are often cooked in a curry and served with local bread in simple eateries: it is proper Goan soul food. I have reduced the amount of curry to make this aadmaas a stickier, finger-licking experience. Some people add sugar and some don't; it depends if you like a little sweetness in your food. These are great by themselves with vegetables on the side, or bread to mop up the sticky sauce. **Serves 4**

Braised sticky Goan-style pork ribs

Grind together all the whole spices and chillies for the paste until smooth. Tip into a blender and add the ginger and garlic along with the vinegar, salt and a little water to help the blades turn and blend until smooth.

Heat the oil in a large pan over a medium heat. Add the onions, green chillies and some salt. Cook until the onions have deep golden edges, stirring often. Add the ribs to the onions, increase the heat to high and fry for 2 minutes. Reduce the heat to medium, add all the paste and continue to fry for 5 minutes or until the paste has darkened and clings to the ribs, stirring often.

Pour 5cm (2in) of water into the pan, bring to the boil, cover and braise gently until the pork is tender, 40–45 minutes. Take the lid off to evaporate most of the excess water. I like to serve these with just enough sauce to dip into, but not a full curry.

Stir in the tamarind and the sugar, if using, taste and adjust the seasoning. Serve hot with lots of napkins, offering more sliced chilli at the table for your guests to serve themselves.

For the spice paste

4cm (1½in) cinnamon stick or cassia bark

1 tsp coriander seeds

1 rounded tsp cumin seeds

7 cloves

10 black peppercorns

1–3 dried chillies (chiles), deseeded, or chilli (chili) powder to taste

25g (1½ rounded tbsp) roughly chopped root ginger (peeled weight)

9 large garlic cloves

1 tbsp white vinegar

1 tsp salt

For the ribs

1 tbsp vegetable oil

2 medium-large red onions, finely chopped

3–4 Indian green finger chillies (chiles), stalks removed, pierced with a knife, plus chopped chillies to serve (optional)

1kg (2lb 4oz) pork loin (baby back) ribs, separated

1½–2 tsp tamarind paste

½ tsp sugar, or to taste (optional)

This is lovely with plain rice and also with naan and vegetables. It is based on a curry I tried at a famous restaurant in Mumbai and set out to recreate in my kitchen. It is really tasty. The strength of tamarind changes between different brands, so add it judiciously and taste before you add more. You can also add 2–3 handfuls of shredded spinach to make a one-pot meal. **Serves 4–5**

Tangy Hyderabad dal

Wash the lentils well in several changes of water and place in a large saucepan. Cover with about 8cm (3in) of water and bring to the boil. Scoop the scum off the top with a slotted spoon and add 1 tsp salt, the turmeric, ginger and grated garlic. Simmer for 30 minutes or until the lentils are soft and the water is becoming yellow. Add the tomato. Keep giving the pot the occasional stir, especially towards the end as the lentils often sink to the bottom.

Heat the ghee in a small saucepan. Add the cumin and mustard seeds and, once they are popping, add the curry leaves. Give them a few seconds, then add the onion and chillies and cook until the onions are translucent and turning brown on the edges. Add the chopped garlic and stir-fry for 1 minute or until just colouring as well. Pour the mixture into the lentils along with most of the tamarind.

Simmer for a few minutes, then taste and adjust the salt and tartness (tamarind) to taste and stir in the coriander.

125g (⅔ cup) yellow lentils (mung dal)
125g (⅔ cup) split pigeon peas (toor dal)
salt
½ tsp ground turmeric
1 tsp finely grated root ginger
4 large garlic cloves: 1 finely grated, 3 finely chopped
1 large tomato, chopped
2–3 tbsp ghee, or butter with a little oil (the oil stops butter from burning)
¾ tsp cumin seeds
½ tsp brown mustard seeds
12 fresh curry leaves
½ red onion, finely chopped
2–3 green chillies (chiles), stalks removed, either pierced with a knife, or 1–2 chopped for more heat
1½–2 tsp tamarind paste, or to taste
handful of chopped coriander (cilantro)

Lentils and beans

I doubt lentils and beans (pulses) are given as much importance in any other country as they are in India. They are one of the oldest known foods and were woven into the cuisine many thousands of years ago, but are considered as important to the diet today as they ever were. In fact, the Indian phrase dal roti – literally "lentils and bread" – is the colloquial term for a meal.

But while a bowl of lentils is everyday comfort food, this is not the only way in which Indians enjoy them. In fact, the many different ways in which Indians craft these humble ingredients shows the sophistication of the country's cooking. They make bread out of chickpea (gram) flour (see page 196) or raw lentils; cook kebabs held together by roasted chickpea flour; steam, fry or bake light, fluffy, gluten-free cakes (see page 18); form dumplings to cook into a curry (see page 115)… and that's before we even get on to crispy pakoras or poppadoms, sprouted spicy bean salads or stir-fries (see page 34).

On a practical note, Indian lentil and bean dishes can scare people off, as there are so many different types, often sold under a few dialect names. In the recipes in this book, I have made sure to be clear about which lentil I mean, so you should be fine.

I often write recipes for canned beans – as most people I know don't get around to pre-soaking beans – but cooking dried beans from scratch does give you more flavour and better control over their texture. However, the older the bean, the longer they take to cook, so keep an eye on the pot as well as the indicated time in the recipe, and try a bean to make sure it is cooked through before taking it off the heat.

Lastly, lentils and beans are full of goodness in the form of fibre, protein, minerals, iron, folate and magnesium. All of these make them good for our heart, digestion, controlling blood sugar and more. Really, if there is one healthy change we should make to our diet, adding more lentils and beans is it!

One of the only times I saw my father by the stove was when he was telling my mother how to cook this dish, a fish curry he has been eating his whole life. He has so many great stories from his childhood, but one of his favourites is of fishing with his brothers in the river near his home in Punjab and bringing back the spoils. This was the curry they would make with the fish and it was the only one he was particular about my mother cooking his way. It is easy and tasty and perfect with Simple, Perfect Rice (see page 189). **Serves 4**

Dad's fish curry

Grind together the cumin, peppercorns, mustard and coriander seeds until fine.

Blend together the tomatoes and garlic until smooth, add the spice blend, chilli powder and turmeric and blend once again.

Heat 2½ tbsp of the oil in a large non-stick karahi, wok or saucepan. Add the dried chillies and the fenugreek and mustard seeds. Once the popping starts to die down, add the blended tomatoes and some salt. Cook over a high-ish flame, stirring often, until the paste releases oil, 10–12 minutes.

Move the paste to the side of the pan, or remove it entirely, and add the remaining oil. Add the fish and fry for 1–2 minutes on each side. Then add enough water to cover the fish (around 500ml/2 cups), the green chillies and coriander and bring to the boil. Cook for 4–5 minutes or until the fish is cooked through. The sauce will continue to thicken as it sits, because the fish absorbs the liquid. In the end it should be only a little creamy but not thick.

For the spice blend
¾ tsp cumin seeds
⅓ tsp black peppercorns
1½ tsp brown mustard seeds
1 tbsp coriander seeds, or ground coriander

For the curry
3 large tomatoes, quartered
15 large garlic cloves
½ tsp chilli (chili) powder
¾ tsp ground turmeric
4 tbsp vegetable oil
2 dried chillies (chiles)
¼ tsp fenugreek seeds
¼ tsp brown mustard seeds
salt
600g (1lb 5oz) firm white fish, cut into steaks (Dad's favourite is rohu, or sea bream)
3 Indian green finger chillies (chiles), stalked removed, pierced with a knife
2 handfuls of coriander (cilantro) stalks and leaves, roughly chopped

Chinese immigrants came to India in the eighteenth century to work at the ports of Calcutta, Madras and Mumbai... and India got its first taste of Chinese food. Restaurants catering for the immigrants started to fuse Indian ingredients with the food their customers wanted, and Indo-Chinese dishes were born. This is one of those dishes and a favourite with vegetarians. It gives a lovely sticky, spicy, sweet sauce that clings to the paneer. The green chillies here add depth but not too much heat as they do not cook too long and the seeds and membranes remain inside. This is the only dish in which I use ketchup, as it works, adding a sweetness and some vinegar. I like to serve this with some rice, but to be honest, I am also really happy to eat it on its own. **Serves 3–4**

Indo-Chinese chilli paneer

Blend the garlic and ginger until smooth, adding a little water to help the blades turn. Separately, mix together the tomato ketchup, tomato purée and dark soy sauce. Lastly, stir together the cornflour, flour and 4–5 tbsp water and gently stir in the paneer.

Heat 2 tbsp of the oil in a large, wide frying pan over a medium heat. Add the paneer in a single layer; if it does not fit, brown it in 2 batches (don't throw away the flour slurry). Fry the paneer, turning, until golden on all sides. Take out of the pan and place on kitchen paper to blot off excess oil.

Add the remaining oil to the pan. Add the garlic and ginger paste and cook over a medium heat until it is just starting to colour. Add the onion, pepper, chillies and a small splash of water to stop the garlic from darkening too much. Stir-fry for 4 minutes or so, splashing in a little more water if the garlic is getting dark.

Add the paneer, the ketchup mixture, vinegar and 2 tsp of the flour slurry, with a good splash of water from the kettle. Stir-fry until the whole thing comes together into a lovely sticky sauce. Add the spring onion, season to taste and serve.

4 large garlic cloves
12g (1 scant tbsp) roughly chopped root ginger (peeled weight)
2 tbsp tomato ketchup
2 tbsp tomato purée
3 tbsp dark soy sauce
3 tbsp cornflour (cornstarch)
2 tbsp plain (all-purpose) flour
300g (10½oz) paneer (ideally fresh), cut into 2.5cm (1in) cubes
4 tbsp vegetable oil
1 small red onion, cut into 2.5cm (1in) cubes
1 small green or red (bell) pepper, cut into 2.5cm (1in) cubes
3–6 green chillies (chiles), stalks removed, pierced with a knife
1½–2 tsp white wine or rice vinegar, to taste
1 large spring onion (scallion), thinly sliced on the diagonal
salt
¼ tsp freshly ground black pepper, or to taste

Most different regions of India have their own way of cooking minced meat. They are all delicious in their different ways. In my home it was cooked Punjabi-style with some peas; my friend's mother made it with fewer spices and added potatoes. Both were equally delicious. Here is a version from Kerala, with little flakes of coconut, and you can cook this with minced beef as well. It is lovely with the crisp Flaky Malabar Paratha, but equally tasty with Simple, Perfect Rice, Tamil-style Lemon Rice, or Spiced Andhra Tomato Rice (see pages 195, 189, 192 and 191). **Serves 4–6**

Malayali stir-fried minced lamb with coconut

Start with the spice paste. Grind the cinnamon, cloves, cumin, coriander, fennel, black pepper and curry leaves to a fine powder. Now blend them with the ginger, garlic, and coconut until you have a coarse paste – you may need to add some water to help the blades turn. I like my coconut to be quite chunky, so sometimes add it towards the end.

Heat the oil in a karahi or non-stick saucepan, add the curry leaves and follow after a couple of beats with the onion and chillies. Sauté until the onion is browned on the edges, add the lamb and brown for 4–5 minutes. Once it starts to release water, cover and cook for 15 minutes, stirring occasionally.

Add the coconut paste, tomatoes and salt and stir well to mix, then cover and continue cooking for another 8–10 minutes or until the lamb is soft. Taste and adjust the seasoning and serve hot.

For the spice paste
2.5cm (1in) cinnamon stick
4 cloves
¾ tsp cumin seeds, or ground cumin
1 tsp coriander seeds, or ground coriander
¾ tsp fennel seeds
¾ tsp black peppercorns, or freshly ground black pepper
10 fresh curry leaves
20g (1½ tbsp) roughly chopped root ginger (peeled weight)
4 large garlic cloves
60g (⅔ cup) fresh chopped or grated coconut, or 30g (2 tbsp) desiccated coconut

For the lamb
1½ tbsp vegetable oil
10 fresh curry leaves
1 red onion, finely chopped
2–4 Indian green finger chillies (chiles), stalks removed, pierced with a knife
500g (1lb 2oz) minced (ground) lamb
2 tomatoes, chopped
salt

For me, this is soul food; the curry we had every week at home. It is the one that my friends and I would descend upon after returning to my family home after a night out (yes, I left home very late in life) with some buttered toast. I still remember that fondly, 20 years on.

This curry is light and almost broth-like. Using whole chicken joints is important, as it really rounds out the flavours of the dish. If you have a friendly butcher, ask him to joint and skin chicken pieces for you; if not, you can find packets of thighs or drumsticks in the supermarket. Buy tomatoes that are not too sweet, so they add a tartness that will balance the onions and give body to the curry.

The secret to any well-cooked curry is the cooking of the masala – slowly and over time is the best way – so be a little patient; it is worth the effort. Eat with Chapati (see page 194). **Serves 6**

Mum's Punjabi chicken curry

Using a little water to help the blades turn, blend together the ginger and garlic. Set aside.

Heat the oil in a large non-stick frying pan. Add the whole spices and, once they have sizzled for 10 seconds, add the onion and cook until golden brown. Add the chillies and the ginger-garlic paste and sauté until the moisture has evaporated and the garlic has had a chance to fry and starts to colour. Add the tomatoes, salt and ground spices and sauté for 6–7 minutes.

Add the chicken and stir it in the masala for 4–5 minutes – this will help develop the flavours a little more. Add enough water to come halfway up the chicken, bring to the boil, then cover and cook over a low heat for 20–30 minutes or until the chicken has very nearly cooked through.

Uncover the pan, turn up the heat to high and reduce the liquid until it is thick and creamy, stirring often as you do. This will help the sauce become homogenous as well as deepen its flavours.

Now add enough hot water to create a sauce the consistency of light cream. Taste and adjust the seasoning, stir in the coriander and serve.

20g (1½ tbsp) roughly chopped root ginger (peeled weight)
10 large garlic cloves
5 tbsp vegetable oil
5cm (2in) cinnamon stick
2 large black cardamom pods
4 green cardamom pods
4 cloves
2 bay leaves
1 medium-large onion, finely chopped
1–2 green chillies (chiles), stalks removed, pricked with a knife
3 tomatoes (not too ripe), blended
salt
2 level tbsp ground coriander
2 tsp ground cumin
½ tsp ground turmeric
¼–½ tsp chilli (chili) powder
1½ tsp garam masala (fresh if possible, see page 113)
750g (1lb 10oz) bone-in skinless chicken pieces
large handful of chopped coriander (cilantro)

This is a typical, warming dish from Punjab and we have been making it at home for as long as I can remember. The whole spices give a wonderful depth and roundness to the flavour. The coriander brings a lightness and freshness to the dish that is so much more than a garnish. Eat this with Chapati or a rice pilaf (see pages 194 and 189)... or even, as we sometimes did at home, with rounds of hot buttered toast: truly moreish. You can find Indian bay leaves in Indian stores or online; don't use regular bay leaves instead as they taste different. **Serves 5–6**

North Indian lamb and potato curry

Finely grate the ginger and garlic.

Heat the oil in a large non-stick saucepan. Add the whole spices and bay leaf and stir for 10 seconds before adding the onions and some salt. Fry until well browned, 8–10 minutes. Add the lamb and stir-fry for 2–3 minutes before adding the ginger-garlic paste. Cook, stirring, for a couple of minutes or until the liquid in the pan has evaporated and the garlic is cooked.

Add the tomatoes, ground spices and a little more salt. Bring to the boil, then reduce the heat to medium-low and simmer, covered, for 50 minutes. Keep an eye on it and give it an occasional stir, splashing in a little boiling water if it gets dry.

Uncover the curry, increase the heat and stir-fry the lamb in the sauce until it has darkened and the oil has come to the surface; this can take up to 10 minutes. Add enough water to cover the lamb and return to the boil. Add the chillies and potatoes, cover again and cook for 15 minutes.

The meat should be tender and the potatoes cooked (check with a small sharp knife, it should go through easily). Taste and adjust the seasoning. Crush the dried fenugreek leaves in your fingers and sprinkle in along with the coriander, give the pot a stir and serve.

2.5cm (1in) root ginger (peeled)
9 large garlic cloves
4–5 tbsp vegetable oil
2 black cardamom pods
4 green cardamom pods
4 cloves
½ tsp black peppercorns
1 dried Indian bay leaf
2 onions, finely chopped
salt
800g (1lb 12oz) cubed lamb, bone-in if possible
4 medium-large tomatoes, blended
½ tsp ground turmeric
1 tbsp ground coriander
1½ tsp ground cumin
1 rounded tsp garam masala (fresh if possible, see page 113), or to taste
1–3 Indian green finger chillies (chiles), stalks removed, pierced with a knife (optional)
2 potatoes, peeled, cut into 5cm (2in) chunks
1 tsp dried fenugreek leaves, *kasturi methi* (optional)
good handful of chopped coriander (cilantro) leaves and stalks

Turmeric

There was a time when I had to explain to people why Indians include turmeric in almost all their dishes. Now most people already know. It is one of the healthiest and easiest ingredients to include in everyday meals, with lots of benefits.

Turmeric is a vibrant yellow-orange rhizome. It is mostly used ground, but can also increasingly be found fresh. It is a spice that Indian mothers add to their foods and into the milk for their children because their mothers did, and they have learned it is very good for them. This general inheritance of ancient knowledge is a big part of Indian food and its relationship with Ayurveda, the ancient Indian science of how to live to be healthy.

Another common practice was putting a turmeric and chickpea (gram) flour paste on a bride before she was married; this was said to give her glowing skin on the day of her wedding. Wounds were healed by putting a paste of turmeric or even turmeric powder straight on top. Now of course, with all the research that has been done on the healing properties of turmeric, it all makes sense. Turmeric is anti-bacterial and anti-viral, which is why it would be put on wounds and in our milk.

It is also anti-inflammatory and, while little inflammations in the body are fine, beneficial even, more chronic inflammations are associated with most of the major illnesses. Curcumin (the active compound in turmeric) is known to help inflammation at a cellular level, so is really good in our never-ending quest to kill free radicals and never age.

Having said all this, the amounts you need to remain healthy means that turmeric needs to be your best friend and not a passing fancy. Also, curcumin is hard for the body to absorb, so, to help absorption, it should be taken with black pepper and ghee or oil, as curcumin is fat-soluble. Therefore, there is no better place for turmeric than in an Indian meal, and no better meal for your health… Enough said: I rest my case!

Once I got married, my mother-in-law made me her, proper Rajasthani, version of a dish my own mother's family had been cooking for years. Rajasthan is a desert, so you can't always find fresh ingredients and dishes would often be conjured up from larder ingredients. These little dumplings (gatta) based on my mother-in-law's are cooked in a simple but incredibly tasty yogurt and tomato sauce which is based on the one my mother made. It is fun to make, easy, cooks in 20 minutes and is exquisite. I crave it if I haven't eaten it for a while. I eat this with Simple, Perfect Rice (see page 189); any other dish just distracts me from my pleasure. **Serves 3–4**

Rajasthani c   ry

Knead together all the ingredie   e gatta
of a medium firmness.   (1 cup) chickpea (gram) flour

Bring a large pot (around 700   sp vegetable oil, plus more to
it. Meanwhile, rub some oil on   e the dumplings
the dough and roll into long r   nded tbsp plain yogurt
isn't important; mine are usua   salt
                                                           cumin seeds
Add the dumplings to the boi   ground turmeric
they will rise to the surface. R   p chilli (chili) powder,
cooking water into a measuri   to taste
(¼–½in) thick "coins".   p carom seeds

For the curry, blend the tom   the curry
                                                          edium-large tomato
Heat the oil in a non-stick saucepan over a low heat. Add the cumin   2 rounded tbsp plain yogurt
seeds and, once they redden (around 20 seconds), add all the   2 tbsp vegetable oil
remaining spices and cook gently for another 15 seconds. Add the   ¾ tsp cumin seeds
tomato mixture and a little salt and cook, stirring, until it has reduced ½ tsp ground turmeric
to a thick paste and you can see oil droplets coming out at the sides,   ¼ tsp chilli (chili) powder
around 10 minutes.   1½ tsp ground coriander
                                                                          ⅓ tsp garam masala (fresh if
Add the gatta and 500ml (2 cups) of their cooking liquor into the   possible, see page 113)
pot. Bring to the boil and simmer for 6–7 minutes. The gravy will   handful of coriander (cilantro)
be only lightly creamy and will thicken further as it sits so, if need be,   leaves (optional), to serve
add a little more of the gatta "stock". Taste and adjust the seasoning
and serve hot with rice or Indian breads, scattering with coriander if
you like.

Accompaniments and sides

An accompaniment sounds like an afterthought but, in India, it can make or break a meal. Crisp, soft flatbreads give texture and contrast to a curry. Rice with lentils makes the protein in the lentils complete. Raita adds a creamy tang and often crunch to tender-cooked vegetables and meats, while chutneys bring life to anything they are paired with. Indian cuisine is ancient and, though it continues to evolve, the basic principles will always give you a tasty meal.

Carbohydrates are a cornerstone of Indian food and, as a Punjabi, flatbreads are my thing. Breads are more than sustenance; they add texture, earthy flavour, interest and bite. The dough can be as simple as flour and water, cooked without oil or salt, but they can also be elaborate creations stuffed with vegetables, or soft, flaky parathas as rich as puff pastry. As a guide, stuffed breads are eaten alone or with yogurt, while simpler breads work with thicker curries. I often suggest that you start by pairing breads and dishes from the same region, as they just work, and move on from there if you like.

Rice is the other staple, and the curries that go with it are typically thinner and brothier, so all the grains are lightly coated. India has so many varieties of rice, but in the West you mostly find the fragrant, long-grained basmati. Shorter-grained, thicker rices are used in the south of India and add a nutty texture.

A raita is a seasoned yogurt given some texture by a vegetable – cooked or raw – or even fruit or nuts. It is a staple in Northern provinces, where there is a thriving dairy industry. The South of India has a raita equivalent of sorts, made from blended coconut, spiced, seasoned and often made with fruit; pineapple is a favourite. There are also crunchy South Western Indian salads which are delicious; some people add them to yogurt for a hybrid dish and it works really well. You really can use anything you want in a raita: try cooked potatoes, fried okra, orange segments, beetroot (beet), aubergine (eggplant), herbs, walnuts and even coconut.

Another favourite is chutney. In India, it is a requirement and not an option. Tandoori food without a green herby chutney, a chaat without tamarind chutney, or a dosa without coconut chutney… each is unthinkable! Indian chutney is used as a dipping sauce, is drizzled or dolloped over streetfood dishes, or eaten with a meal. Each has a clear flavour profile from its main ingredient. I have included the most popular in this chapter, as well as those I just love the most. Chutneys are also probably the most versatile preparations in the kitchen. I see them as a shot of flavour and often make them to freeze, perfect for adding flavour to any dish.

Lastly, good-quality, fresh-ground spices make a tasty dish. Old ground spices retain their staleness even when cooked into a dish. Whole spices ground in batches and a fresh, homemade garam masala make a lot of difference to a dish. These home-ground spices will retain their flavours for months and are really worthwhile.

There are so many variations of this along the coast of India, but the one I am wedded to is a typical Tamil-style chutney soured with yogurt and lemon juice rather than tamarind. I make a big batch of this (without the tarka and yogurt) and freeze it in smallish portions; when I am making some south Indian food, I defrost it and add the tarka and yogurt at that point. It tastes as good as fresh. **Makes around 240ml (1 cup)**

Coconut chutney

For the chutney
50g (¼ cup) chana dal
1 dried chilli (chile)
75g (¾ cup) fresh grated coconut (find frozen packets in Asian supermarkets, or fresh pieces in mainstream supermarkets)
1 tbsp lemon juice
5g (1 tsp) chopped root ginger (peeled)
2 tbsp plain yogurt
salt

For the tarka
1 tbsp vegetable oil
1–2 dried chillies (chiles)
1 tsp brown mustard seeds
12 fresh or dried curry leaves

In a dry frying pan over a medium heat, dry-roast the chana dal with the dried chilli until golden and aromatic; this takes 2–3 minutes. Add enough water to cover the base of the pan so the lentils can absorb the water and soften; leave to cool. When it's cool, blend it with the coconut, lemon juice and ginger until smooth-ish; it can have some texture to it. You will need to add some water (around 75ml/⅓ cup). Season to taste with salt.

Now for the tarka. Heat the oil in a small saucepan or tarka pan. Add the dried chillies and mustard seeds. Once these are popping, add the curry leaves, then add the tarka to the coconut with the yogurt. Taste and adjust the seasoning.

A really delicious seasoning for those who like heat and flavour. I highly recommend it on the Maharashtra's Ultimate Potato Burger (see page 14). This can be kept in the fridge for weeks. **Makes about 6 tbsp**

Dry garlic chutney

1 tsp vegetable oil
1–3 dried chillies (chiles), or chilli (chili) powder, to taste
7 large garlic cloves, peeled
2 rounded tbsp desiccated coconut
salt
2 tbsp roasted peanuts

Heat the oil in a small pan. Add the chillies and, once they darken a little, add the garlic and cook for 1 minute or until just lightly coloured on all sides. Add the coconut and a little salt. Stir until the coconut is golden.

Pour into a good mortar and pestle (or grinder), with the peanuts, and pound to a fine powder. Season to taste.

This is like Indian ketchup... but is not reserved for children. It is sweet and tangy but has a fair amount of spice from the black pepper. We eat it on a lot of our chaats, as a dipping sauce for samosas and dhoklas, and I use it in sweet, sticky marinades as well. It takes a little while to make but lasts for weeks in the fridge and longer in the freezer. **Makes about 180ml (¾ cup)**

Proper date and tamarind chutney

75g (2¾oz) dried tamarind
100g (½ cup) dates
125g (generous ½ cup) sugar, or to taste
½–¾ tsp freshly ground black pepper
¾–1 tsp salt, or to taste
1½–2 tsp roast and ground cumin
  seeds, or to taste (see page 184)

Place the tamarind and dates in a saucepan. Cover with water and a lid and cook over a gentle heat for 20–30 minutes or until it is pulpy and mashed. Pour into a large sieve over a large bowl and force through as much as you can, then, when cold enough to handle, collect the pulp in the sieve and squeeze it – still over the bowl – to remove all the bits. Discard the fibres and stones.

Pour the tamarind and date liquid back into the pan with the remaining ingredients and cook for 1 hour or so. It will cook down, become glossy and syrupy. Taste and adjust the sugar, seasoning and spice. Pour into sterilized jars and, once cool, place in the fridge. Or leave to cool, then divide into portions and freeze.

To sterilize jars

Preheat the oven to 140°C/275°F/gas mark 1. Place just-cleaned jars on a foil-lined shelf in the middle of the oven and leave for 20 minutes or until completely dry. Remove with oven gloves and fill the hot jars with hot chutney, or leave both to cool before filling. (The important thing is that they should be at the same temperature.)

While this is typically served with Nepalese momos (see page 20), this chutney is so tasty that you will find yourself dipping into it often, as the flavours go with and spice up so many different dishes and snacks. **Makes about 200ml (¾ cup)**

Spicy charred tomato chutney

2 large tomatoes
½ tsp cumin seeds
small handful of sesame seeds
1 rounded tsp finely chopped garlic
1 tbsp finely chopped root ginger
1 tbsp vegetable oil
handful of chopped coriander (cilantro)
chopped green or red chilli (chile), to taste

Roast the tomatoes until charred; I do this on my griddle pan, turning the tomato as each side chars. Peel off the skins and discard.

Dry-roast the sesame and cumin seeds over a gentle flame until the sesame seeds are golden. Grind or pound these into a powder.

Chop up the tomato and blend coarsely with the sesame seed mixture. Fry the chopped garlic and ginger in the oil for 40 seconds. Add to the tomatoes with the coriander and as much chilli as you like, and season to taste.

This is a lovely, versatile chutney that is tangy and herby rather than sweet. It is the cornerstone of all north Indian snacks. We love it with our samosas, bhajis, pakoras, kebabs and most other things. There are many variations: some will add a little sugar, some raw garlic, and others yogurt. This is how we like it in my family and it is a perfect base from which to experiment if you want. **Makes 200ml (¾ cup)**

This is that lovely, refreshing sweet mint chutney that is often on your table as you start your meal. I always dip my popadums into it, but also eat it with all my tandoori food. It is a lovely, creamy, sweet, spicy and lightly sour chutney that goes really well with all grills, barbecues and many snacks. **Makes 150–200ml (about ¾ cup)**

Tangy herb chutney

60g (3 cups) coriander (cilantro) leaves and
   some stalks
2 tbsp lemon juice, or to taste
20g (¾ packed cup) mint leaves
25g (¼ cup) pistachios (shelled weight)
salt
½ garlic clove (optional)
4 tbsp water

Blend all the ingredients until smooth and creamy; it might take a minute or so.

Taste and adjust the seasoning and tang (lemon juice) to taste.

Keep in an airtight glass jar in the fridge or freeze until ready to use.

Minted yogurt chutney

7g (1½ tsp) mint leaves, chopped
20g (¾ packed cup) coriander (cilantro) leaves
   and stalks, chopped
½–1 Indian green finger chilli (chile), stalk removed
2 tsp sugar
1 tsp lemon juice, or to taste
150g (⅔ cup) plain yogurt
⅓ tsp roast and ground cumin seeds (see page 184)
salt

Blend everything together until smooth, then taste and adjust the seasoning.

Paneer is a white cheese with a dense, crumbly texture that works wonderfully with Indian spices. It is full of virtues: packed with protein, vitamins and minerals, and so tasty that even carnivores love it. **Makes 325–350g (12oz)**

Homemade paneer

2 litres (2 generous quarts) whole milk
salt
200–250g (¾–1 cup) plain yogurt, or
  3–4 tbsp lemon juice

Bring the milk to the boil in a heavy-based saucepan. Once it starts to boil and rise up, boil it to thicken slightly for 5 minutes or so. Salt lightly.

Stir in 200g (¾ cup) of the yogurt or 3 tbsp of the lemon juice and keep stirring; the milk should separate into curds and whey. The liquid should be clear and slightly green-tinged. Add tmore yogurt or lemon juice if it doesn't split. Remove from the heat.

Line a large sieve with clean muslin (cheesecloth) or a J-cloth and place in the sink. Strain the cheese into the sieve and run some cold water through it, to remove excess sourness. Wrap the cheese in the muslin, ball and squeeze out as much water as you can. Place on a sturdy board over a surface onto which water can drain. Fill the cooking pot with water and place on top of the wrapped cheese, making sure it is balanced properly. The cheese should look like a round, fat block.

Leave to set for 45 minutes, or less if you want a looser texture. (A denser texture stays intact during cooking, but looser paneer is softer.) Once set, remove the paneer from the muslin and cut into pieces. Store unused pieces in the fridge in water and cover. You can also freeze it in an airtight container (although the texture will change slightly and become crumbly). Defrost thoroughly before use.

A lovely, refreshing raita that is really versatile, lovely with Indian food, great with grilled meals and very refreshing just with some naan or pitta bread. **Serves 4**

Classic cucumber and mint raita

1 tsp cumin seeds
200g (½ large) cucumber
400g (1½ cups) Greek yogurt
salt and freshly ground black pepper
8g (1½ tsp) shredded mint leaves
small splash of milk and/or a pinch of sugar (optional)

Place the cumin seeds in a small dry frying pan over a medium heat and stir just until they turn a shade darker and smell aromatic. Remove and grind to a powder in a mortar and pestle or a spice grinder.

Grate the cucumber on the coarse side of a box grater. Squeeze out all the excess water and place the cucumber in a large bowl.

Add three-quarters of the cumin and all the remaining ingredients except the milk or sugar and stir well to mix. Taste and adjust the seasoning, adding the milk or sugar if the raita tastes too sour for you. Sprinkle over the remaining cumin and serve chilled.

I once held a flatbread-making class on the banks of the Yarra in Melbourne and made this raita for people to try with their breads. They said it was one of the best they had ever had. It will perk up even the simplest meal. **Serves 4**

Pomegranate and mint raita

1 small pomegranate
450g (1⅘ cups) plain yogurt
¾ tsp roast and ground cumin seeds (see page 184)
good pinch or 2 of sugar, depending on the tartness of the yogurt
small handful of shredded mint leaves
salt and freshly ground black pepper

Quarter the pomegranate and extract the kernels straight into a bowl, making sure you peel off all the white pith, as this is bitter.

In another bowl, stir the remaining ingredients. Add enough pomegranate to balance the raita and stir well. Season to taste and serve.

I have have been eating garlic-flavoured Greek yogurt with my food ever since I visited Greece years ago. Add as much or as little garlic as you like, or to suit what you are eating it with (spiced meats can take more than vegetables). **Serves 4**

Spinach and garlic raita

75g (2½ packed cups) baby spinach
450g (1½ cups) Greek yogurt
salt
lots of freshly ground black pepper
½–1 garlic clove, to taste, finely grated
½–¾ tsp roast and ground cumin seeds (see page 184)

Place the spinach in a saucepan with 2–3 tablespoons of water and cook until soft, 1–2 minutes. Drain and squeeze out the excess water.

Stir the spinach into the yogurt with the salt, pepper, garlic and cumin. Serve chilled.

One of our favourite raitas and among those we probably eat the most at home. It is refreshing, crunchy and flavourful. **Serves 4**

Tomato, onion and cucumber raita

1 ripe tomato, chopped into 1cm (½in) dice
¼ red onion, finely chopped
90g (3oz) cucumber (about ¼ cucumber), diced the same size as the tomatoes
large handful of chopped coriander (cilantro)
¾–1 tsp roast and gound cumin seeds (see page 184)
450g (1⅘ cups) plain yogurt, whisked until smooth
good pinch of sugar, or to taste
salt and freshly ground black pepper

Stir all the ingredients together and season to taste. Add more sugar if your yogurt was particularly sour.

Raita

A raita is a seasoned and lightly spiced yogurt side dish or accompaniment. It always contains a fruit or vegetable for flavour, texture and – basically – direction. The added fresh ingredient is up to you, but the most common is one or more of a combination of crunchy salad-like ingredients and herbs, such as tomato, cucumber, onion, carrot, coriander (cilantro), mint, dill or curry leaves. The spice is often roast and ground cumin seeds or brown mustard seeds, but I have also used the ground-up seeds of black cardamom pods. Cooked vegetables also make delicious raitas: try crispy okra, wilted spinach, potatoes or beetroot (beet). Some cooks also add fruit in season: try pomegranate seeds, orange segments, mango or even banana. The fresher the yogurt, the less sour your raita will be. If the yogurt is very sour, you can add a little sugar or even a splash of milk to the dish to temper that.

Growing up, my mother always made a batch of fresh yogurt at home, and the end of the last batch would be the starter for the next. It was the way she grew up, it was frugal and practical. Until recently I did the same… but life got too busy. I have to say, I still miss the freshness of that yogurt.

To make your own yogurt, heat up some whole milk until just frothing, stirring very often so it doesn't catch on the pan and burn. Allow to cool until it is just warm. Stir it into some bought yogurt – it's important that you like the taste of the one you use – and whisk to combine. Wrap the pan in a dish towel and place in a warm oven (I warm it up, then turn it off before adding the pan). Make sure the oven isn't so hot that the towel catches fire! Leave to set for 4–5 hours, or overnight. The longer you leave it, the tarter it will become, but you do need it to set. Then place in the fridge, cover and chill. There might be a pale liquid that rises to the top; just drain this off.

I generally visited India in the winter, when carrots, beetroots, moulis (radishes) and a host of other lovely vegetables are in season. Meals were – and still are – served with thinly sliced vegetables, seasoned with salt and chilli powder and doused in lemon juice. They were addictive – even as a child I enjoyed them. This chopped salad is known as a kachumber, great with all Indian meals but also with barbecues. **Serves 4**

This koshimbir is a really lovely, nutty, crunchy salad that is cooling and perfect with spicy meals or grilled meats. You can also make it with cucumber instead of carrot. Leave out the yogurt and add a squeeze of lemon juice, if you prefer. **Serves 2–3 (can be easily doubled)**

Indian chopped salad

2 ripe vine tomatoes
120g (about ⅓) cucumber (I like to keep the skin on)
3 small radishes
¼ small red onion, finely chopped
1 Indian finger green chilli (chile), deseeded and finely chopped (optional)
1 tbsp lemon juice, or to taste
⅓ tsp roast and ground cumin seeds (see page 184)
1 scant tbsp dried mint
handful of chopped coriander (cilantro) leaves
salt and freshly ground black pepper

Chop the tomatoes into small dice. Slice the cucumber lengthways, discard the seeds and cut into small cubes the same size as the tomatoes. Do the same with the radishes.

Toss together all the vegetables and chilli, if using, with the lemon juice, the roasted ground cumin, dried mint, coriander and seasoning. Serve.

Maharashtrian carrot and yogurt salad

1 small carrot, finely chopped or coarsely grated, water squeezed out
120g (½ cup) Greek yogurt
½ small Indian green finger chilli (chile), finely chopped
handful of chopped coriander (cilantro)
1 tbsp desiccated coconut
1 tbsp salted peanuts, roughly chopped or pounded
salt and a good amount of freshly ground black pepper
½–¾ tsp sugar, or to taste
1 tsp vegetable oil
⅛ tsp brown mustard seeds
⅛ tsp cumin seeds
4–5 fresh or dried curry leaves

Add the carrot to the Greek yogurt with the chilli, coriander, coconut, peanuts, seasoning and sugar.

Heat the oil in a small pan over a medium-high heat and, once hot, add the seeds; as they pop, reduce the heat and cook until the popping is dying down. Add the curry leaves, cook for another 5–6 seconds, then pour into the yogurt. Stir all together, taste and adjust the seasoning and sugar, and serve.

Rice is one of the simplest and quickest grains to cook, yet it is so easy to get it wrong and so – unfortunately – people can steer away from making it at home. The technique for cooking it is actually very easy and not so different from pasta; you just need to know when to stop the cooking. This is the way we have always made it in my family. Just increase the quantities as you need; the method will remain the same. **Serves 1**

Simple, perfect rice

70–80g (scant ½ cup) good-quality white basmati
  rice per person

Wash the rice really well in several changes of water until the water runs clear and all the starch has been removed. To do this, I place the rice in a saucepan and pour over water. Swirl it well with your fingers to dislodge the starch on the grains and pour off the water. Repeat until the water is clear.

Now, in the saucepan, cover the rice with at least 8cm (3in) water.

Bring to the boil, then reduce the heat and simmer (as you would pasta) for 6–8 minutes. Try a grain: it should be cooked through; if not, cook for another minute and check again. Drain the rice through a sieve, then return it to the pan over a medium-low heat to dry off any excess water, around 1 minute.

Turn off the heat, cover and allow to steam for 8–10 minutes.

A colourful, lovely rice pilaf that goes with everything and smart enough to cook when you have friends over. You can also make it just with peas, just with carrots, or even add some chopped green beans. **Serves 4–6**

Fragrant pea and carrot pilaf

350g (2 cups) basmati rice, well washed
4 tbsp vegetable oil
1¾ rounded tsp cumin seeds
10cm (4in) cinnamon stick
4 cloves
2 black cardamom pods
2 bay leaves
1 onion, sliced
1 small carrot, cut into 1cm (½in) cubes
120g (¾ cup) frozen peas, defrosted
salt
¾ tsp garam masala (fresh if possible, see page 113)

Place the rice in a saucepan and pour in at least 8cm (3in) of water to cover. Bring to the boil and simmer for 6–8 minutes. Try a grain at 6 minutes: it should be nearly soft. If not, cook for another minute and taste again. Drain the rice in a sieve, then pour it back into the pan. Cook for another 40 seconds over the heat to dry off any excess water and then turn off the heat, cover the pot and let the rice steam for 8–10 minutes. It should now be fully cooked through.

Heat the oil in a wide frying pan and add the spices and bay leaves. Cook until the cumin is aromatic, around 20 seconds. Add the onion and fry until just soft. Add the carrot, peas and salt, stir and cook for 2 minutes. Finally, cover and cook for 3 minutes.

Uncover the rice pan: there should be no water left (if there is, cook it off over a high heat). Add the rice and garam masala to the frying pan and stir well. Taste, adjust the seasoning and serve.

I tried this as part of a lovely vegetarian thali at Chutneys restaurant in Hyderabad. It was really flavourful and moreish – I could eat a whole plate of it! Clearly, I had to try and recreate it. I'm not convinced that mine is as good as theirs, but I could still eat a plateful of it, so I'm happy! There is very little water used here, so it takes longer to cook than some of my other rice dishes. I add Bengal gram (chana dal) – even though it wasn't in the original – because I like the bite and roasted flavour, but it is optional, in case you don't have any at home. This rice is great by itself, but also lovely with any curry. **Serves 4 with a main course**

Spiced Andhra tomato rice

Wash the rice well, until the water runs clear, then leave it to soak while you cook.

Heat the oil in a non-stick saucepan that has a lid. Add the whole spices, curry leaves, bay leaf and chana dal and, once they have sizzled for 10 seconds, add the onion. Add 1 tsp salt and cook until the onion smells cooked and has darkened slightly.

Meanwhile, blend the tomatoes with the garlic, ginger and powdered spices until smooth. Add to the cooked onions, bring to the boil and cook until completely reduced and the masala releases oil back into the pan; around 15 minutes.

Drain the rice, add to the pot and stir to mix well.

Add 300ml (1¼ cups) water, taste and adjust the seasoning (it should be a little salty); bring to the boil. Then reduce the heat to its lowest, cover and cook very gently for 13 minutes. Unlike other rice dishes, I do like to give everything a gentle stir… but only once.

Taste and see if it is cooked through. If not, leave it for another minute or so. Once it is done, take it off the heat but leave covered for another 5 minutes. Fluff through with a fork and serve.

180g (1 cup) basmati rice
3 tbsp vegetable oil
6 cloves
5 green cardamom pods
2.5cm (1in) cinnamon stick
10 fresh or dried curry leaves
1 dried bay leaf
1 tbsp chana dal (optional)
1 small onion, blended or grated to a paste (don't worry if there are a few large bits)
salt
2 large-ish tomatoes, quartered
2 garlic cloves
5g (about 1 tsp) finely chopped root ginger (peeled weight)
½ tsp ground cumin
½ tsp fennel seeds, ground
½ tsp garam masala (fresh if possible, see page 113)
¼ tsp chilli (chili) powder, or to taste

This is such a delicious and versatile rice from the south of India that, even though I have written the recipe before, I wanted to include it in this book. The Tamils would make this rice and take it on long journeys, as it keeps well in a container and is so satisfying. This updated version is perhaps simpler but very tasty and works with coconut curries, tomato-based curries, dal or grilled chicken or fish. The lentils and seeds give it texture and flavour but do not overpower the flavours of the rice. The tang is really delicious and lifts this rice dish from a throwaway accompaniment to a deserving star. If you wanted to add a few more elements, try fresh grated coconut or lightly roasted and chopped peanuts. **Serves 4**

Tamil-style lemon rice

Bring a large pot of water to the boil over a high heat. Add the drained rice and return it to the boil. Cook for 6–7 minutes, then check a grain; it should be done but not mushy.

Drain the rice, then return it to the pan over a low heat. Partially cover and dry off the excess moisture for a minute or so. Cover and leave undisturbed for 5–10 minutes or until you are ready to cook. (You can make this up to this stage earlier in the day, or even use yesterday's boiled rice leftovers.)

Heat the oil in a large non-stick frying or sauté pan. Add the seeds, lentils and chilli, reduce the heat and cook until the popping of the seeds subsides and the lentils are golden. Add the curry leaves and follow 5 seconds later with the ginger, salt and turmeric. Fry for 40 seconds or so.

Add the lemon juice and cook for another minute before adding the rice and coriander leaves. Stir the rice with a fork to mix well. Taste and adjust the seasoning and serve.

220g (1¼ cups) basmati rice, washed well in several changes of water and soaked as far in advance as possible
4 tbsp vegetable oil
2 tsp brown mustard seeds
1½ tsp cumin seeds
1½ tbsp urad dal (split and skinned black lentils)
1½ tbsp chana dal
1 tbsp split chana dal
1 dried red chilli (chile), halved
12 fresh curry leaves
10g (2 tsp) finely chopped root ginger (peeled weight)
salt
⅓ tsp ground turmeric
3½–4 tbsp lemon juice, or to taste
handful of chopped coriander (cilantro) leaves

Neer dosas are very light, very thin rice pancakes from Mangalore, with a good rice flavour. They are dipped in curries and eaten and I really enjoy them. The trick to making them is to keep the batter very thin: neer means "water" in their dialect. You can add 2 tbsp fresh grated coconut to the batter, grinding it with the rice for a more substantial dosa.

These are lacy looking and have holes, so don't expect an even surface. And they remain snow-white, so do not try to brown them. Lastly, they tend to stick when hot, so do not pile them on top of each other when they're ready. **Makes 9–10 (can easily be doubled)**

Skinny rice dosas

Once the rice has been soaking for a few hours, blend it with the water and salt until really thin, watery and smooth. Expect this to take 4–5 minutes. It should flow like water so, if it seems too thick, add a little more.

Heat a non-stick frying pan over a medium heat. Place the oil in a small bowl. Spear the onion with a fork through the rounded side. Dip the flat end into the oil and wipe the surface of the pan with the oiled onion.

When the pan is hot, pour in 80ml (⅓ cup) of the batter, tip the pan to allow the excess to spread everywhere but it shouldn't have complete coverage, it will be a bit lacy. Cook until the underside is crisp and the upper side has lost its moist look, 4–5 minutes. Gently ease your spatula underneath and loosen the dosa, then flip it and cook it for 30 seconds on this side to help it dry out.

Take the dosa out of the pan, fold it in half and then into quarters.

Make the next one, stirring the batter first to make sure the solids are not collecting at the bottom, and wipe the pan with the onion again.

Repeat to make the rest.

90g (½ cup) basmati rice,
  soaked for 3 hours
300ml (1¼ cups) water
⅔ tsp salt, or to taste
2 tbsp vegetable oil
½ small onion

Chapati, phulka and roti are all names for the same basic, everyday wholewheat flatbreads many Indians eat with their meals. The breads add a chewy, nutty element and are also a perfect way of enveloping your curry and vegetables. They really do add to the meal and are quick and easy to make. At home we like to cook them so they puff up and one side crisps up – as in the method below – but if that seems a bit too much, just cook them on both sides until they have some little brown spots on them. You can find chapati (atta) flour in most large supermarkets, but if you can't get a hold of any, use equal quantities of wholewheat and plain flour. The breads can be made in advance and reheated, wrapped in foil, in a medium oven. We never put salt in our breads as they are used to mop up well-seasoned sauces. **Makes 10 (can easily be doubled)**

Chapati, phulka and roti

Sift the flour and salt (if using) into a bowl and make a well in the centre. Slowly drizzle in most of the water and, using your hand, draw the flour into the centre, mixing all the time. You may not need all the water, as flour absorbs different amounts of water depending on its age and the moisture content in the air. The dough should be just slightly sticky and almost squeak as you knead it, but it will firm up.

Knead for 8–10 minutes or until the dough seems elastic and most of the joints and lines have worked themselves out. If it feels hard, sprinkle some more water over it and knead it in. Then place in a bowl, cover with a damp dish towel and leave for 30 minutes. By now it should be soft and easy to work with.

Divide the dough into 10 equal portions and roll each into golf ball-sized rounds; then cover again with a damp dish towel. Flour the work surface and rolling pin. Roll each ball into thin 13–15cm (5–6in) circles. The best way to do this is to keep rolling in one direction, turning the dough a quarter of a circle after each roll to get a round shape.

Heat a tava (or non-stick frying pan) over a high heat until quite hot. Toss a chapati from one hand to the other to remove any excess flour, then place on the tava. Reduce the heat to moderate and cook until small bubbles appear on the underside, 10–20 seconds, then turn. Cook this side until it too has small, dark beige spots.

The best way to puff a roti is to place it directly over an open flame (with the brown spotted side on the top), using tongs. It will puff immediately; leave it there for 10 seconds until dark spots appear. I like to move it around the flame, for even puffing up. Place on a plate. Repeat with the rest. If you only have an electric hob, press a cooked roti down gently on the heat source; as you press one area the rest should puff up. Then tackle the next area. This way the roti should puff up all over.

Keep the bread warm by wrapping in a napkin or some foil while you make the rest and leave in a low oven until ready to eat.

300g (2⅓ cups) chapati flour (or half wholewheat and half plain/all-purpose flour), plus more to dust
salt (optional)
200–240ml (⅞–1 cup) water

This is a rich, flaky paratha that is one of Kerala's most famed breads. Muslim bakers brought it to this mostly rice-eating part of India and it was quickly adopted as a local favourite. They are lots of fun to make and really delicious to eat. The breads go with everything but are particularly good dipped into a curry, especially if that curry is hearty and meaty. You can make these in advance and reheat, wrapped in foil, in a medium oven. **Makes 4 (can easily be doubled)**

Flaky Malabar paratha

Mix together the dry ingredients. Make a well in the centre and add the egg and most of the milk. Mix well to form a slightly sticky dough. Turn out on to a work surface and knead until you have a soft, if a tiny-bit-sticky, dough. Rub oil over the ball, cover with a little oiled kitchen paper and let it rest for 10–15 minutes.

Divide the dough into 4 equal portions and form each into a ball. Leave to rest under the oiled kitchen paper for another 30 minutes.

Lightly oil a large work surface. Taking one piece of dough at a time, roll it out as thin as you can into a rectangular shape. It should be elastic and pliable and fairly easy to roll; don't worry about any little tears. Now loosen the edge from the work surface and gently pull it, to stretch a little more, from each side. You should be able to stretch it out to a rectangle of about 28–31cm (11–14in).

Drizzle over around 1 tsp of oil, sprinkle all over with a light dusting of flour and then salt. With a light hand, fold, fan-like, into thin pleats. It doesn't have to be at all neat. You can also cut strips along the length of the rectangle and gather and stack these up as you go. (Either pleat or cut the breads, though – don't do both!) Coil these strips around themselves, cut sides up, tucking the ends underneath. Pat down and set aside, covered, as you do the rest. Leave to rest for 20–30 minutes.

Now roll each out into a thin circle. Heat a tava or frying pan. Place a piece of dough on the surface and cook for 20–30 seconds or until the underside looks dry. Turn over and drizzle 1 tsp of oil around and on top of the bread. Fry until the underside is golden and crisp, then flip and repeat, drizzling with a little more oil. Set aside.

Cook the remaining breads in the same way. Once 2 of them have cooked, put one on top of the other, place them on kitchen paper and scrunch it up into a ball; this helps open the layers and makes them flaky. Keep warm and serve as soon as possible.

150g (1¼ cups) plain (all-purpose)
   flour, plus more to dust
1 tsp sugar
½ tsp salt, plus a little more to
   use in the layers
1 egg
2–2½ tbsp whole milk
vegetable oil, as needed

India has so many wonderful breads, but this is one of my favourites. It isn't too indulgent, nor too simple and plain. The flavours add a lot to the bread and eventually to the meal as well, although the bread is often the main star of a meal and simply eaten with yogurt and pickles. I add yogurt to the bread as it makes it a softer dough, but you can leave it out (it isn't traditional) and add a little more water instead. Another regular addition is dried fenugreek leaves; if you have some, add 1 tbsp. **Makes 6 large flatbreads**

Missi roti

Mix together all the dry ingredients and spices. Add the oil and yogurt or water and knead well to a semi-hard dough. Leave to rest for around 20 minutes.

Make 6 large balls with the dough. Lightly oil a work surface and roll out each bread into a circle about 13cm (5in) in diameter. Make the rest if you have the space, or make half now and repeat with the next batch later.

Make on the hob

Heat a tava, flat griddle or frying pan over a medium-high heat. Put in a bread ball. Once the underside has dried out, 30–40 seconds or so, flip over and drizzle with ½–¾ tsp oil. Flip again and cook on both sides, pressing down gently until both have golden-brown spots on them. Brush with a little soft butter and wrap in foil.

Repeat with the remaining breads and serve, or keep warm by stacking them on each other and keeping them in foil, wrapped in a dish towel.

Make in the oven

Preheat the oven to 190°C/375°F/gas mark 5 and place a baking sheet on the middle shelf.

Wet your hands and pat the breads with water on one side. Place on the hot baking sheet, water side up. Cook until you have golden spots on the top. The base should also be cooked by now, but if you aren't sure and it looks very pale, you can flip these and cook for another 20–30 seconds on the underside.

Serve hot, smeared with the softened butter.

150g (1¼ cups) chapati flour
60g (½ cup) chickpea (gram) flour
½–1 small green finger chilli (chile), finely chopped or sliced
3 tbsp finely chopped red onion
3 tbsp finely chopped coriander (cilantro)
¼ tsp cumin seeds
¼ tsp carom seeds
¼ tsp coriander seeds
⅛–¼ tsp chilli (chili) powder
¼ tsp ground turmeric
½ tsp garam masala (fresh if possible, see page 113)
1 tbsp vegetable oil, plus more to work the dough and cook the breads
4–5 tbsp plain yogurt or water (see introduction above)
unsalted butter, softened, to finish

Naan is the quintessential restaurant bread, lightly puffed and a little charred in places, reminding you of the tandoor it was cooked in – light, chewy and pliable. You can make naans at home and they are really delicious and soft. Increasing the oven temperature will give it some charring... but be careful not to overcook them.
Makes 6 medium-large naans

Naan

300g (2⅓ cups) plain (all-purpose) flour,
  plus more to dust
1½ tsp sugar
⅔ tsp salt
1 tsp easy-bake dried yeast
1 tbsp vegetable oil, plus more to work the dough
4 tbsp plain yogurt
140ml (½ cup) water
unsalted butter, softened, to finish

Mix together all the dry ingredients. Add the liquid ingredients and knead well for 6–8 minutes or until it is soft and springy. Oil the dough ball, place it in a bowl, cover with a dish towel and plate and leave in a warm-ish or draught-free place for 30–45 minutes. When it has risen, it should be light and soft; you should almost be able to pat it into its shape.

Preheat the oven to about 240°C/475°F/gas mark 9, or as high as it will go. Place a large baking sheet on the upper shelf.

Divide the dough into 6 balls and, taking one at a time, pat and roll out into a tear-shaped or oval naan bread, 1–1.5cm (½–¾in) thick. Repeat with another 2 and place these 3 on the hot baking sheet.

Bake until the upper surface has some lovely golden spots, 2–3 minutes, then flip and bake another 30–40 seconds or so until the other side has also cooked through. Brush the top with butter, place in foil to keep warm, and repeat with the others. Serve hot.

Poppadoms and papads

There is no definitive answer as to the difference between a poppadom and a papad. I am in the habit – rightly or wrongly – of calling the roasted version a papad and the fried version a poppadom. Maybe this is because we have always had flame-toasted papad at home. However, British curry houses – and the British – refer to them as "poppadoms", and they are always fried in the UK. Either way, they are addictive, thin crispy discs mostly made from types of lentils, though some Indian regions make them with potatoes and rice. (I have even noticed that some storebought brands make them with flour.)

In England, restaurants will often give you a basket of fried poppadoms as you order food, but many Indians don't eat poppadoms before a meal. We Punjabis eat ours with a meal, while my Rajasthani in-laws will finish their meal with them, as they are believed to aid digestion, or also make amazing curries out of them. Goans soften and stuff them with a variety of fillings before deep-frying them; perfect bar food! And one of the tastiest poppadom experiences I have had is in a Mumbai restaurant, where it was served hot with a mix of toppings.

Poppadoms come in many sizes and with a variety of different spice flavourings. Whichever way you enjoy them, don't forget them when eating an Indian meal; they definitely add to the experience.

Indian breads

India has an amazing array of breads: from simple flatbreads made with plain or wholemeal flour and water, to elaborate flaky breads enriched with milk and ghee; leavened breads that are simple, or elegant saffron versions; everyday stuffed breads; more elaborate stuffed breads made with naan dough layered into a soft flakiness, such as Spiced Potato-stuffed Spiced Potato-stuffed Amritsari Kulcha Bread (see page 150); multi-grain breads such as Missi Roti (see page 196); breads made from chickpea (gram) flour or from cornmeal; breads that are pan-fried and those that are deep-fried… I could go on.

Indian cuisine has always grown richer by learning techniques from her many rulers and settlers and, when it comes to breads, we owe a lot of gratitude to the appetites of the Moghuls (and Arab traders and settlers), who brought with them a deeper understanding of bread-making and its secrets. With them came tandoori breads, leavened breads, almost puff pastry-like flatbreads such as Flaky Malabar Paratha (see page 195), and large soft breads such as romali roti, so fine and thin that they are named after a handkerchief. The earliest mentions of these types of breads came from travellers, who wrote about their visits to the Delhi Sultanate, where they ate fine tandoori-baked breads at breakfast with their kebabs.

Also noteworthy when talking about breads are the baking traditions and techniques brought to India by the homesick Portuguese, who ruled over Goa for hundreds of years. They missed their breads (then, India had no ovens) and sent for their own bakers, who set about teaching locals how to craft breads from local ingredients, including semolina and coconut toddy. This extended to cakes and biscuits (although again most of these were made on the hob), including a local version of a Christmas cake. The legacy of the Portuguese can be seen in cities around the South Western coast, in the form of pau (the Portuguese word for bread is *pao*). Pau looks like a well-risen square burger bun. These are now served with butter alongside curried vegetables and spiced minced meat, as well as being used as a burger bun with local potato cakes… that might sound heavy, but it is divine (see page 14).

Indian food is designed to be eaten with a starch and – even when tasting a dish – a chef might remind you to taste it with rice or a bread, to appreciate the real flavour. For most, a proper Indian meal would be incomplete without the familiar chew of the flatbread that so perfectly complements the flavours and textures of the soft meaty curries, vegetables and lentils and – helpfully – scoops them up into the perfect mouthful as well!

Desserts

In India, every happy event, prayer ceremony or festival is celebrated with something sweet, so it is no surprise that the nation has a fairly crushing sweet tooth. There are two types of "desserts": home-style sweets rustled up by Mum; or those made by a professional *halvai* (most of these fall under the collective banner of *mithai*). I do love Indian desserts, and I feel bad for them that they are relegated to a small chapter at the end of this book when they hold far more symbolic importance in India than that of a mere full-stop at the end of a meal.

Home-style desserts tend to be quite simple, made with humble ingredients such as grains, vegetables, dairy products, coconuts, nuts, dried fruits… even lentils and spices. If this doesn't sound immediately appealing, may I remind you of a few perennial Western favourites: pumpkin pie, carrot cake, bread pudding and custard tart. There is a lot to love. Indian sweets are generally cooked with varying amounts of sugar or jaggery and ghee, and often flavoured with cardamom or saffron.

Diwali, in our home, always meant there would be a type of kheer (milky, cold rice pudding, sometimes with added carrots, mangoes, or other ingredients); prayer ceremonies would be accompanied by the simple-but-delicious semolina halva. While Indian desserts can be a bit sweet, one doesn't normally eat a lot, and only after a meal; teatime treats and breakfasts tend to be savoury.

Mithais require more technique and experience to get them just right, and recipes tend to be kept under lock and key by the professional halvais, as they are the key to the success of the family business. Indians take their sweet specialities very seriously, with people travelling to eat the best or freshest. When I first visited my new in-laws in Kolkata, I mentioned that I would love to try the very seasonal Bengali speciality of set, sweet date syrup yogurt at some point. At breakfast the next morning, a clay pot containing thick-set yogurt of a faint caramel hue was on the table. It was delicious, creamy with a light tang and with lots of natural datey-caramel flavour and sweetness. The clay pot draws the liquid from the yogurt, so it thickens as it sets. Apparently, my in-laws had sent someone out at 5am to wait in a queue for it, as they sell out by 10am!

Mithais are as beautiful and well presented as home-style desserts are rustic, but Indians have an abiding love for both. However, Indian desserts do divide people, even families; my children thankfully love them, my husband not at all. So, in this chapter, along with some traditional dishes, I have also used Indian flavours and ingredients in more familiar ways that I hope will appeal to a Western palate, but still round off an Indian meal really well. I have included some healthy desserts and some gluten- and carb-free sweets, which might sound like a compromise but – I promise you – still deliver.

As children, we used to love watching the Wimbledon finals with our cousins. It was often the case that we would support opposing players and the atmosphere would get very competitive. There was always a crescendo of noise and tension as the match came to its end; feathers would be ruffled and egos bruised. My aunt (or mother, I can't remember) would bring out this halva and we would bury our differences in the delicious, humble but comforting pudding. It is simple, but we all love it. This recipe is based on my mother's recipe and the chickpea flour is a secret – really tasty – addition. It is a quick-to-make pudding in a world where desserts can take hours. You can spruce it up (if you double the recipe) by spooning it into a small cake tin and allowing it to set. Cut into squares or diamonds and serve with some plain or spiced ice cream. **Serves 3–4 (in small bowls; double the quantities for larger portions)**

Comforting semolina halva

Add the saffron to the hot water and leave to infuse.

Place a small saucepan over a medium heat. Add 1½ tbsp of the ghee and the semolina. Roast until it is a medium golden colour, around 6–7 minutes. Add the chickpea flour and continue cooking the semolina until it is well roasted and has darkened a little more, another 2–3 minutes. It should be quite deeply golden.

Add the sugar and stir for 30 seconds or so. Add the saffron water and cardamom and cook for a few more minutes, or until it all comes together and leaves the sides of the pan.

Stir in the remaining ½ tbsp ghee, the nuts and raisins, take off the heat and serve hot or warm.

pinch of saffron threads
200ml (⅚ cup) hot water
2 tbsp ghee
50g (¼ cup) semolina (ideally medium-grained)
1 rounded tbsp chickpea (gram) flour
45g (¼ cup) sugar, or to taste
small pinch of ground cardamom
15g (⅛ cup) roasted cashew nuts
small handful of raisins or sultanas

This dish is known as "the sweet made from apricots" and was brought to Hyderabad with the ruling Moghuls. At first glance it may seem too simple to grace Moghul tables, but apricots were local to where the Moghuls came from in central Asia, so they were dried and brought across the continent. They were then cooked unadulterated, served only with some nuts and cream (both expensive ingredients) – no fillers, no filters; the ultimate show of wealth. This dish is still popular in Hyderabad, a southern Indian city, but people now add saffron or cardamom pods to the apricots; I prefer them without. I have added pieces of filo for texture; it works so well with the soft, sweet apricots and the cool cream. This dish is definitely more than the sum of its parts. I don't like my desserts too sweet, but add the extra sugar if you aren't like me. I like the complexity of roasted salted pistachios here, but you can use plain. **Serves 4–5**

Glazed apricots with pistachios and filo

Earlier in the day, or even the evening, before you want to make the dish, soak the apricots in a bowl with plentiful water to cover.

When you are ready to cook, drain the apricots, place them in a saucepan and cover with 5cm (2in) water. Bring to the boil, then reduce the heat and simmer gently for 25–30 minutes, or until soft, adding the sugar halfway and turning the apricots in the syrupy water as they soften, to make sure they are all a little glazed. Remove from the pan with a slotted spoon.

There should be 4–5 tbsp of syrup left in the pan. If it seems watery, boil it down a little; if it is too thick, add a spoon or so of boiling water.

Preheat the oven to 200°C/400°F/gas mark 6. Roughly tear the filo into large pieces, I try to tear them into odd-sized shards of maybe 5cm (2in) maximum, but it isn't important to be precise. Melt the butter and toss the filo shards in it. Line a baking sheet with baking parchment and scatter the filo pieces over it. Bake in the hot oven until golden, giving the bits a stir every now and again to make sure there is even browning. It only takes a few minutes. Take out.

When ready to eat, lightly whip the cream. Shake or sprinkle a little icing sugar over the filo. Make sure all the apricots are glazed; if necessary, dip them in the syrup.

Place the apricots in the bottom of 4–5 small dessert dishes, or a serving bowl. Top with a good dollop of the cream, pile over lots of filo shards so that they are slightly vertiginous, sprinkle over the pistachios and drizzle over the extra syrup. Serve.

200g (1 generous cup) dried apricots
2½–3 tbsp sugar, to taste
2 filo (phyllo) pastry sheets
2 tbsp unsalted butter
200ml (⅚ cup) double (heavy) cream
2 tbsp icing (confectioner's) sugar
handful of roasted pistachios, salted or plain, roughly sliced or chopped

India is embracing a new trend, modernizing its cooking through Michelin-star dining, molecular gastronomy, or mixing Western techniques and dishes with Indian ingredients. I suppose I am no different in my culinary curiosity: I love mixing and matching my Eastern and Western culinary influences and, when I get an idea, I need to pursue it to a conclusion. This dish is the result of that exploration... with a very happy result. Green mangoes are unripe and have a lovely fresh acidity – less sharp than lemon and slightly fruitier. This recipe is in the tradition of the classic French tarts that I love so much, with the added bonus of the health properties of this fruit, so dessert is not *all* bad! This will not be as smooth as a classic lemon tart, as the mango has some texture, and it will also be lighter as the filling is as much green mango as it is cream. **Makes a 23cm (9in) tart (serves 8)**

Green mango curd tart

Start with the pastry. In a large bowl, or using a food mixer, cream together the butter and sugar until light, pale and creamy. Add the 2 egg yolks and stir well to mix them in. Add the flour and salt and rub into the mixture with your fingers, as you would with a crumble. Once the texture is sandy and crumbly, add 1 tbsp water and bring together into a ball with your hands. If it does not come together, add another 1 tbsp water. Make sure the pastry isn't too crumbly; the heat from your hands will help it come together but do not over-work it, or it will be tough. Form it into a ball, wrap in cling film (plastic wrap), pat into a large disc and refrigerate for 30 minutes.

Once the dough has chilled, roll it out (still on the cling film) as evenly as possible into a round about 3mm (⅛in) thick. Using the cling film, transfer to a 23cm (9in) loose-bottomed tart tin and place inside, gently pushing the corners in the tin so that it fits completely and comes up the sides. Cut off the excess pastry by rolling the pin over the tin. Prick the base of the pastry all over with a fork, line with foil and fill with baking beans, dried beans, or raw rice. Place in the fridge for 20 minutes, and preheat the oven to 160°C/325°F/gas mark 3.

Bake for 12 minutes, then carefully lift out the foil and beans and bake for a further 20–25 minutes or until it is a lovely golden colour.

Peel the mangoes and cut the flesh away from the stone. You need about 220g (8oz) flesh – please weigh it. Blend it with the eggs, sugar, melted butter and cream until smooth. Strain about a quarter of it and remove the fibres of the mango left in the sieve (don't take them all out as they add texture). Skim off any bubbles from the surface.

Brush the inside of the pastry with some of the reserved egg white and place back in the oven for 1 minute. Now reduce the oven temperature to 120°C/250°F/gas mark ½. Fill the tart with the filling and gently place in the oven, or fill while it is on the shelf already. Bake for 25–30 minutes, or until just set on the surface, with a slight skin. Remove from the oven and leave to cool. Once cool, place in the fridge for 2 hours. Dredge with icing sugar and serve as is, or with crème fraîche.

For the pastry

120g (½ cup) unsalted butter, at room temperature

75g (½ cup) icing (confectioner's) sugar, sifted, plus more to serve

2 egg yolks, plus 1 egg white

250g (2 cups) plain (all-purpose) flour

good pinch of salt

For the filling

400–450g (14oz–1lb) whole green mangoes (if they are small, use the higher amount as there is more wastage)

2 large eggs

180g (scant 1 cup) sugar

30g (2 tbsp) unsalted butter, melted

220ml (scant 1 cup) double (heavy) cream

crème fraîche, to serve (optional)

India has a whole genre of sweet desserts which were once made in the home, but are now mostly made by specialized halvaies – Indian pâtissiers. Gulab jamun are one of India's favourites: little syrupy doughnuts made from thickened milk instead of flour and soaked in sugar syrup rather than stuffed with jam or sweetened in the batter. I use dry milk powder which I rehydrate, not the traditional thickened, solidified milk, as that takes too long and needs too much attention to make. There are only two tricks to getting these doughnuts right: the right consistency of dough (not too soft, not too hard); and frying them over a very low heat so they cook all the way to the centre, stirring the oil almost continuously so they brown evenly. I like them warm as they will be softer, and you can reheat them in their syrup, but you can equally eat them cold. Serve as they are, or with a little ice cream. **Makes 18 (serves 1–2 per person)**

Sticky saffron dumplings

Mix together the dry ingredients for the dumplings. Spoon in the ghee, yogurt and milk. Mix well with your hands to bring the dough together; it will be moist. Set aside.

For the syrup, heat the sugar, water and saffron together in a saucepan, stirring to help the sugar dissolve. Once boiling, simmer for around 3–4 minutes, then turn off the heat. Add the rose water, using the smaller amount first and tasting until you have a strength you prefer.

Meanwhile, pour 8–10cm (3–4in) of oil into a medium-large karahi, wok or wide saucepan. Heat gently.

Divide the dough in half. Wet some kitchen paper and place on top of the dough you aren't working with. Grease your palms well with ghee, take half the dough and form it into 9 small balls; I like to make them slightly oval rather than round, but you can shape them as you like. The surfaces should be smooth and crack-free. (If the dough is too soft to shape, add a little milk powder.) Repeat to make and shape the remaining dumplings.

To check if the oil is ready, put a tiny pinch of the dough into the oil. It should only sizzle very slightly. When it is ready, add the balls in batches so as not to crowd the pan, stirring the oil as you put them in. Cook over a gentle heat, stirring and turning them very often for even browning, they should take 15–17 minutes per batch to reach a lovely golden brown. Once done, take them out with a slotted spoon and place straight into the syrup. Repeat with the next batch.

Cover and leave to soak for 2 hours, or overnight, in the fridge. They should last 10 days or more. Serve as they are, or sprinkle them with sliced pistachios.

For the dumplings

400ml (1⅔ cups) whole milk powder (measure it in a measuring cup), plus more if needed
100g (½ cup) plain (all-purpose) flour
⅔ tsp baking powder
2 tbsp ghee, plus more to form the dumplings
5 tbsp plain yogurt
5 tbsp whole milk
vegetable oil, to deep-fry
sliced pistachios, to serve (optional)

For the syrup

450g (scant 2 cups) granulated sugar
650ml (2⅔ cups) water
2 good pinches of saffron threads
½–1 tsp rose water, depending on strength

This classic sweet and salty mint lassi is very popular in the northern Punjab, where field workers used it to replenish their bodies with both salt and sugar while refreshing and cooling themselves with buttermilk, mint and cumin seeds. Easier to digest than milk and yogurt, buttermilk is considered a light and healthy way to get your dairy, but most of us now blend together yogurt and water until we have a light frothy lassi. I always thought it would be a good idea to make lassi floats – the slight sourness of the lassi had to be a great foil for the ice cream – and they really work a treat; complex but easy, and more sophisticated than a soda float. These are now a favourite fun dessert when friends come round with their children. For an extra dimension, make it into a falooda, a colourful part-drink, part-dessert that you eat with a spoon. It is delicious, and lighter than many puddings! **The classic lassi serves 1; the floats/faloodas make 6**

Classic sweet and salty mint lassi

180g (¾ cup) plain yogurt, or, if it is quite tart, add
  just 150–160g (⅝ cup) and adjust at the end
120ml (½ cup) water
2 tsp sugar, or to taste
pinch of salt
⅓–½ tsp roast and ground cumin seeds (see page 184)
2 tbsp shredded mint leaves, or dried mint, crumbled
  in to taste
crushed or shaved ice, to serve

Blend together the yogurt, water, sugar, salt, cumin and half the mint. Stir in the remaining mint, taste and adjust the sugar and yogurt. Chill, before serving with crushed or shaved ice.

Lassi floats and faloodas

480g (2 cups) chilled plain yogurt
400ml (1⅔ cup) water
5 tbsp sugar, or to taste
crushed ice, to serve
6 small scoops of ice cream (try lemon curd,
  strawberry, vanilla, fruity frozen yogurt or
  any other that you love)

Blend together the yogurt, water and sugar until light and frothy. Adjust the sugar to taste; the amount you need depends on how sour the yogurt is.

Pour into glasses furnished with some crushed ice.

Add small scoops of your chosen ice cream or frozen yogurt. Leave for 5–10 minutes, then serve.

For the falooda

Soak 5 tbsp black chia seeds in milk to cover for 20 minutes, or until they plump up. Cook 80g (2¾oz) falooda sev noodles (Indian cornflour noodles available in Indian stores), or some thin rice noodles, according to the packet instructions. Mix these together with a little coloured syrup (grenadine, violet or more traditional rose syrup). Divide the noodles and syrup between glasses; there should be 1 tsp-ish of the syrup per glass. Add the chia seeds on top, then follow the recipe above.

Like everyone, I have friends who prefer to avoid gluten and dairy and when they come round I need to have a special think about what to serve them. This is one of the desserts I will go to when mangoes are in season; easy, tasty and lovely after an Indian or spicy Asian meal. It is based on a popular Chinese dessert we see a lot in India – simply a light mango cream with lovely gelatinous tapioca pearls, mango and freshly grated coconut. This recipe proves again that, if you have good-quality, inherently tasty ingredients, you don't need a lot more to make a fabulous dish. This is one of my summer favourites, really refreshing. It thickens overnight, so you may want to thin it with a bit of milk (and then taste for sweetness) before serving. You can also add some chia seeds. **Serves 4–5**

Chilled mango, coconut and "pearl" puddings

Soak the tapioca pearls for 20 minutes. Bring a large pot of water to the boil – you do need lots of water. Add the drained tapioca pearls, bring to the boil, cover and cook for 14 minutes. Take off the heat and leave to finish cooking for another 10 minutes, or until they are translucent, or almost so. You want to keep an eye on them as if they over-cooked, they become gluey. Pour straight into a sieve and place in a large bowl of cold water. Set aside.

Slice the cheeks from the mangoes and scoop out the flesh, keeping all the juices as you work. Set 1 cheek aside. Put the rest into a blender with the juices. Remove the skin from the stones and try to get as much flesh and juice off it as you can; put this straight into the blender. Add the coconut cream, the smaller amount of milk and the sugar. Blend until smooth. Add the rest of the milk if it is thick (you might even need more, it all depends on the juiciness of the fruit), until the texture is like double (heavy) cream. Add half the coconut. Taste and adjust the sugar to taste.

Add the cold pearls to the mango cream and chill until ready to eat.

When you are ready to serve, chop the reserved mango into slivers. Pour the mango cream into small bowls, pile some of the mango in the middle, top with the remaining fresh coconut and crispy tapioca pearls, if you like, and serve chilled. Or, for a more graphic look, place the tapioca in the glasses, spoon over the mango cream, swirl in a little sweetened coconut cream and garnish with any of the options.

Crispy tapioca pearls

Soak an extra 1 tbsp of tapioca pearls, then dry on kitchen paper. Heat 1½ tbsp flavourless vegetable oil in a small pan, tilt the pan to collect the oil on 1 side and add the tapioca. Cover immediately with a lid as they will try and jump out. Cook for 1 minute or until crispy, drain and place on kitchen paper to blot off excess oil. Leave until ready to use (you can make this a day ahead). I leave these unsweetened, but you can candy them as well, in the same way as you would nuts.

60g (2¼oz) large tapioca pearls, soaked for 20 minutes
2 large ripe Alphonso (ideally) mangoes
125ml (½ cup) coconut cream, or to taste
175ml–200ml (⅔–⅚ cup) whole chilled milk, plus more if needed
2–3 tbsp sugar, or to taste
5 tbsp grated fresh or frozen and defrosted coconut, chilled

Optional garnishes
crispy tapioca pearls (see below)
crystallized rose petals
flaked roasted almonds
fresh coconut shards
mango wedges

Most Diwalis, my parents threw a party, and Mum always made an Indian dessert to end the meal. Kheer was one of her regular choices; it is cooling, light and normally just a small bowl hits the spot. There are a lot of different types of kheers (carrot, mango, orange, beetroot, pumpkin), but rice is the most traditional. We always eat this chilled, so it is made the night before, which is so helpful. But when I was filming, the (non-Indian) director insisted it was his favourite Indian dessert... but that he only ever ate it warm. I'm not sure if this was a British rice pudding/Indian kheer hybrid – or if there are others who eat it warm – but I leave you to decide how to eat yours. If you are serving it warm, you can reduce the amount of sugar to taste (chilled foods need that bit more). **Serves 4–5**

Classic Indian rice pudding

Heat the milk in a heavy-based saucepan over a low heat, bringing it to a simmer. If the heat is too high, the milk will rise in the pan. Simmer for a few minutes, stirring often, then add the rice. Cook gently, stirring often, for about 1 hour, or until the rice is soft. Stir often, scraping the base of the pan to make sure the milk does not catch.

About two-thirds of the way through, add the spices and condensed milk and continue cooking until the rice is soft and the milk has thickened. It will continue to thicken as it cools.

Once cool, chill in the fridge overnight.

Stir in half the nuts, sprinkle with the remaining nuts and a little more saffron, if you like.

1 litre (4 cups) whole milk
2½ tbsp basmati rice, washed well and soaked for 1 hour
large pinch of ground cardamom, or to taste
pinch of saffron threads, plus more to serve (optional)
6 tbsp condensed milk
10 almonds, blanched and finely chopped
10 unsalted pistachios, finely chopped

These little bites of sweet deliciousness are loved all over India. They are often made at parties, especially in the winter when it is cold outside. My version is lighter, not too sweet, crispy on the outside and soft within. The pancakes come together in less than 10 minutes, so are perfect for those of us in a hurry, or with last-minute friends arriving.

These would normally be glazed in a sticky syrup. I have added sugar to the batter so they don't need it, but I do like the sheen, so I make some up and brush it over the top. They also work really well as a side to Classic Indian Rice Pudding or Saffron Yogurt Phirni (see opposite and page 215). I serve them with vanilla, spiced or ginger ice cream, but they also make delicious breakfast pancakes with some fruit and Greek yogurt. **Makes 16 small pancakes to serve 4–5 (can easily be doubled)**

Fennel and cardamom-spiced mini pancakes

Start by making the glaze, if you want it. Heat the water over a medium heat in a small saucepan with the sugar and saffron, stirring to help to sugar dissolve. Simmer until it is syrupy (6–8 minutes). Set aside.

Now for the pancakes. Stir together all the dry ingredients, then gradually whisk in the milk until you have a smooth batter.

Place a large frying pan over a medium heat, add the ghee and enough oil to come 1cm (½in) up the sides. Once hot, drop rounded tsp of the batter into the oil, dropping in as many as you can. You may need to do it in 2 batches (but won't need more oil). Cook until golden brown on the underside, then flip over and cook this side in the same way. Place on kitchen paper to blot off the excess oil.

Spoon some glaze, if using, on to each pancake. Place 3 on each plate with a little scoop of ice cream in the middle. Sprinkle with the nuts and serve.

For the sticky glaze (optional)
120ml (½ cup) water
50g (¼ cup) sugar
small pinch of saffron threads

For the pancakes
100g (¾ cup) plain (all-purpose) flour
2 tsp semolina
⅔ rounded tsp baking powder
1 tsp fennel seeds, coarsely ground
seeds from 2 large black cardamom pods, coarsely ground
3½–4 tbsp sugar
2 round tbsp ground almonds
pinch of salt
80–90ml (⅓ cup) whole milk
2 tbsp ghee
vegetable oil
ice cream, to serve
2 tbsp chopped pistachios and roasted flaked (slivered) almonds, to serve

Phirni is a Northern Indian dessert made from ground rice and milk, lightly flavoured, typically set and chilled in little clay pots. The clay continues to absorb the liquid from the mixture, making the phirni even creamier. I have added yogurt to this recipe, which gives a subtle complexity that I feel really adds to the dish and helps to balance the sweetness of typical Indian desserts. Make these a day in advance. You can set them in pretty little glass bowls or a larger serving dish. When Indian mangoes are in season, I chop some and add them on top; the musky sweetness really works with this dessert. **Serves 4–5**

Saffron yogurt phirni

Soak the basmati for 1 hour in plentiful water, then drain and dry it completely on kitchen paper. Set aside.

Pour 900ml (3⅔ cups) of the milk into a wide, heavy-based saucepan. Add the saffron. Place over a medium heat, then reduce the heat and gently simmer until it has reduced to 600ml (2½ cups). You will need to stir the milk often, scraping the base of the pan to make sure the milk doesn't catch and burn. If the heat is too high, the milk will rise up in the pan and spill, so keep an eye on it.

Meanwhile, set aside 1 tsp of the dried rice and, using a spice grinder, grind the rest to a coarse powder. Set aside.

When the milk has reduced, add the ground rice to the reserved 100ml (⅓ cup) milk and stir well. Pour this straight into the reduced hot milk with the reserved whole rice, stirring so it does not form a clump. Keep cooking and stirring for 10 minutes or so over a medium heat.

Add the sugar, cardamom and saffron and keep stirring until the mixture has thickened, another 5–7 minutes. It will measure around 450–500ml (about 2 cups).

Cool, then stir in the yogurt. Adjust the sweetness to taste, bearing in mind that as it cools the sweetness will be less pronounced.

Pour into individual bowls or a large serving dish, cover with cling film (plastic wrap) and chill overnight in the fridge. Serve sprinkled with the nuts.

40g (around 2 rounded tbsp) basmati rice
1 litre (4 cups) whole milk
4 tbsp sugar, or to taste
¼ tsp ground cardamom
good pinch of saffron threads
2 tbsp thick, set plain yogurt, not too sour
chopped pistachios or almonds, to serve

Saffron

The aroma and flavour of saffron are unmistakeable and loved by so many. The root of the word comes from the Persian *zafran*, attesting to the introduction of saffron into the West (and East). This spice is the stigma in the heart of the saffron crocus flower. It can only be picked by hand, and each flower only yields three strands, so it stands to reason that they are precious, and prized by those who enjoy the musty flavour and unique aroma.

Saffron has always been expensive, so not found in everyday Indian food, but was used judiciously in rich households when guests visited for a special meal. You will still find little traces of saffron-hued rice giving a biryani a golden glow (see pages 111–112), or find a small pinch of the tell-tale red strands stirred into a creamy rice pudding served on Diwali, like slivers of rubies. I had the privilege of tasting delicious saffron tea in Calcutta when visiting my husband's family, and my all-time favourite remains the Indian mithai (sweet) of saffron and rose water-soaked gulab jamun dumplings (see page 207).

Store saffron in airtight containers in the fridge and – as with truffles – pair it with delicate ingredients so as not to drown out its own subtle flavour. Try it in syrups, or anything creamy, rice dishes, yogurts, or even light breads and cakes. Saffron varies in quality depending on how much of the stigma is picked and also where it is grown. I generally always seek out Iranian saffron and look for a deep red colour.

To get the best from saffron, lightly crush it and infuse it in a hot liquid for 20 minutes.

It is true that many Indian desserts can be rich and sweet, but we do have flavoured Indian granitas in the form of *gola*. These are little cups of shaved ice, flavoured with your choice of sweet syrup.

Shikanji is not a typical flavour; it is a popular lemon drink that is sweet, lightly tangy and gently flavoured with roasted cumin, black salt and mint leaves. It is really refreshing and moreish. The reason salt was added was to replenish and rehydrate people who had been too long in the sun; cumin and mint helped to cool the body. If you don't want to add black salt (which has a sulphurous smell, but not taste), you can add a little pink salt, or no salt at all.

This is subtle and delicious and perfect at any time on a hot day. It is always surprising to those who eat it, as it looks so simple, but hides a multitude of subtle flavours. **Serves 4–5**

Shikanji granita with lemon crème fraîche

Pour the water and sugar into a small saucepan and heat, stirring, until the sugar has dissolved. Take off the heat, add half the lemon zest, all the juice, the cumin, salt and mint. Allow to infuse as it cools for at least 1 hour. Fish out the mint and pour into a flattish rectangular freezer-proof container, cover with the lid and place on a flat surface in the freezer.

Every 45 minutes or so, take it out and break up all the crystals forming on the inside by scraping with a fork, making sure you get the sides as well. Repeat every 45 minutes or so, scraping the granita with the fork so it becomes granular, until it is all frozen.

When ready to serve, stir together all the ingredients for the crème fraîche; I like to use the half-fat version to keep the dessert light.

Remove the granita from the freezer and scrape it again to break it back up. Spoon into little glass bowls or glasses, scatter over the shredded mint and stir it in with a fork, spoon over a dollop of the cream and sprinkle with the pomegranate seeds and some lemon zest, if you like. Serve immediately.

For the granita

500ml (2 cups) filtered water
135g (⅔ cup) sugar, or to taste
finely grated zest of 1 unwaxed
  lemon, plus more to serve
  (optional)
85–90ml (generous ⅓ cup) lemon
  juice
¼ tsp roasted and ground cumin
  seeds (see page 184)
¹⁄₁₆ tsp black salt, pink salt or regular
  salt, or to taste
4 mint sprigs, plus more, shredded,
  to serve
good handful of pomegranate seeds,
  to serve

For the lemon crème fraîche

100g (⅖ cup) half-fat crème fraîche
3 tsp icing (confectioner's) sugar,
  to taste

Index

Dedication: To Mahi and Adi, I love you always.

I feel very lucky to have worked with Quadrille for the last ten years. In a world that keeps changing, it is nice to have had the stability and continuity, as well as their support.

Sarah Lavelle, thank you for publishing yet another Indian cookbook and trusting me to bring something new to it. Céline Hughes, I owe you so much for helping shape the book with your calm intelligence. Thank you Helen Lewis for your patience and determination to get the book right. Emily Lapworth, you have designed such a beautiful and vibrant book that evokes India but in such a modern way. I have to say, I think it is the most beautiful of all my cookbooks.

For this I also need to thank Martin Poole for his absolutely stellar photography; Aya Nishimura for styling each dish so that the food jumps out from the page; and Tamzin Ferdinando, you put together an arsenal of beautiful, characterful and colourful props which brought the food and book into context. I feel blessed to have had you all work on this book.

A big hug and love to my formidable literary agent and friend Heather Holden-Brown. You have been with me since the very beginning and have always encouraged and navigated me in the right direction. Your experience is deep and rich yet always on trend.

Thank you also to Lucy Bannell for ploughing through the text with complete efficiency.

A quick mention of the little ones at home. Mahi, you got involved every time baking was required and at the end of a long day in the kitchen, your enthusiasm and efficiency made cooking a pleasure. The pastry for the green mango tart will always be yours, as you made it more times than I did in the end.

To my little one, Adi, thank you for ninja-chopping my mushrooms for the momos and your honest, if deadpan, comments on the dishes you tasted; "yum", "good", "not good" and "mum, this is the worst one of all!" In fact, thank you to all my family for their patience when I am stressed or too busy to have a life beyond kitchen and computer.

On that note, a very heartfelt thank you Alisa Norbury for making sure my family's life doesn't come to a halt when I am knee-deep in spices. You are tireless and reliable and I honestly don't know how my life would function without you!

A quick thank you to my Spice Tailor colleagues in India, Udai, Percy and Vidhu, for helping plan and meticulously organize numerous trips to different regions of India for "work", enabling me to spend days eating proper regional Indian food that have made my recipes be that much more authentic.

Lastly, Adarsh, you continue to encourage and support me in equal measure. Your work ethic is beyond reproach and completely inspiring! Together, we have created so much, life is always exciting and I look forward to what comes next…

Publishing director Sarah Lavelle
Creative director Helen Lewis
Commissioning editor
Céline Hughes
Designer Emily Lapworth
Photography Martin Poole
Food stylist Aya Nishimura
Prop stylist Tamzin Ferdinando
Food stylist for cover and endpapers
Rosie Reynolds
Prop stylist for cover and endpapers
Lydia McPherson
Production Emily Noto,
Vincent Smith

First published in 2017 by
Quadrille Publishing
Pentagon House, 52–54 Southwark
Street, London SE1 1UN

Quadrille Publishing is an
imprint of Hardie Grant
www.hardiegrant.com.au
www.quadrille.co.uk
www.quadrille.com

Reprinted in 2017
10 9 8 7 6 5 4 3 2

Text © 2017 Anjum Anand
Photography © 2017
Martin Poole
Photography on pages 2, 11, 37,
59, 81, 105, 135, 159, 179, 201
© 2017 Issy Croker
Photography on pages 4–9
© Anjum Anand
Design and layout © 2017
Quadrille Publishing

Cataloguing in Publication Data:
a catalogue record for this book is
available from the British Library.

ISBN: 978 184949 563 9

Printed in China